Jamboroo!

Jimbo Wolfe

To Phil,
Here are some fresh ideas
to enliven your journey

Jimbo

Cover design by children's book author Terry Hueffed
Based on a Pixabay picture from Larisa-K.

ISBN-13 978-1546519621

NOTE:

Instead of a traditional Table of Contents, the introduction indicates the title of each essay or sermon, the gist of its contents and its location in the book by page plus occasionally the context that gave rise to it.

Intro: I sing a song of the love of Sprite
           Who dances like a bee.
           She stings and strokes and frees from fright
           And leads me on a spree.
                          --A Song of Love

Jamboroo! A spree. I invite you to join me on a spree. Jamboroo, a variant of Jamboree: celebration. The tale is told of a monk poring over ancient manuscripts calling his brothers round and saying: "Oh No. We got it wrong for centuries. The word is not celibate; it's celebrate!" Received religion is often dour and restrictive while I prefer my religion to be wild and free. Why shouldn't Roman Catholic priests be allowed to marry especially since married priests are customary among Orthodox Christians and even among Eastern-rite Roman Catholic priests in Orthodox countries. Religion enhances celebration of milestones in life, such as birth, marriage, and death, and this use persists even when church attendance and interest in theology atrophies. In a folk tale found in Genesis 2, man waxes poetic about his new mate: "This at last is bone of my bones and flesh of my flesh, and she will be called Woman because she was taken from Man." Jesus commends marriage as two becoming one flesh and he begins his ministry according to John's Gospel by turning water into wine to celebrate a wedding in Cana. New or renewed life is greeted with ceremony, such as baptism or bris (circumcision), and older life expired is memorialized in a traditional funeral with corpse and casket or, increasingly, as belief in afterlife wanes, with a celebration of the life of the person who passed away. Besides individual milestones, we celebrate with jubilation a vision of Jubilee, when equity will be restored, and victories great and small on the long road to liberation, justice, and peace. Science describes. Religion celebrates. That is my dictum. If you want to know when and how our planet and its creatures have evolved, ask a scientist. If you want to celebrate receiving the world from God's hands each year, you need look no further than the responsive reading in Genesis 1. With original blessing rather than original sin, God sees all that she has created and proclaims it very good. In contrast to John the Baptist with his message of judgment and bad news, Jesus proclaims God's inbreaking kingdom and invites listeners to change their minds and embrace this good news. With a reputation for excess, he comes eating and drinking, friend to toll collectors and prostitutes. Jesus is convivial. He has the oil of gladness above his fellows. He comes that the joy of followers might be full, that they might have life and have it abundantly.

Following Jesus does not exclude drawing on elements from other religions besides Christianity. I note five increasingly positive approaches to the plurality of religions: tolerance, respect, cooperation, appreciation, and appropriation. Tolerance may not like a facet of another religion but puts up with it. Respect recognizes that others have a right to their religion but keeps it at arm's length. Cooperation sees enough values in common to work together. Appreciation likes something in another religion. Appropriation takes what it likes and adds it to one's own faith. Taking the best and ignoring the rest, I incorporate elements from seven religions in my own credo. This credo concludes my first book *A Song of Faith* and is repeated and spelled out in the opening essay in this book entitled **Making Peace Among Religions Within Myself** (page 9).

Drawing on the definition of "civil religion" in my second book, *The Kennedy Myth: American Civil Religion in the Sixties*, a review of the US Supreme Court's decision in "Town of Greece v. Galloway" sees the Court upholding the constitutionality and desirability of the practice in Greece NY of having not only ministers from the town's Christian churches but also a Jewish layman, Baha'i leader, and Wiccan priestess offering prayers at the monthly meeting of the Greece Town Council. Ironically, although "nonsectarian" themes from the common values of the civil religion are most relevant and palatable, the non-establishment and free exercise of religion in the First Amendment requires allowing prayers to include elements from distinctive ecclesiastical "sectarian" traditions. The upshot in my review entitled **A Town Called Greece** (p. 17) is an affirmation of pluralism as in "*e pluribus unum*" on the dollar bill: "out of many one," which comports well with my own multi-faith religion.

The attack on the World Trade Center and Pentagon on 9/11/2001 led me to bone up on Islam and write four essays. **Modernity and Islam** (p. 21) presents modernism as elevating egotism, secularism, and scientific rationalism and tracks the modernization and westernization of Egypt displacing Islamic leadership and community with domination and riches confined to a small elite. **Archaic Religion and Islam** (p. 23) presents archaic religion as featuring idolatry, repression, and literalism leading in Egypt to a Fundamentalist reactionary reaction to modernity by moving into poor neighborhoods and excommunicating official leaders looking instead to militant Islamic leaders such as Ayman al-Zawahiri, who supplied the ideology for Osama bin Laden and al-Qaida, which he now heads.

In **9/11: Behind the Veil** (p. 25), I question US innocence, a sentiment echoed recently by President Trump asking "You think our country's so innocent?" After all, my essay points out, the US is the word's sole military superpower with politics and economics based on individual self-interest and corporate maximization of profits at any cost. No wonder that the discontented blame us and lash out in terrorism. Wrote Nancy Gibbs in <u>Time</u>.

> If you want to humble an empire it makes sense to maim its cathedrals. They are symbols of its faith, and when they crumble and burn, it tells us we are not so powerful and we can't be safe. The Twin Towers of the World Trade Center, planted at the base of Manhattan island with the Statue of Liberty as their sentry, and the Pentagon, a squat, concrete fort on the banks of the Potomac, are the sanctuaries of money and power that our enemies may imagine define us. But that assumes our faith rests on what we can build and buy, and that has never been America's true God.

Along these lines, my 9/11 essay concludes and my essay on **Historic Religion and Islam** (p. 26) begins with a plea for historic religion featuring adherence to a transcendent God rather than archaic nationalism or modern individualism, self-control rather than archaic domination or modern license, and symbolism rather than archaic and modern literalism;then it details some of the historic themes in the life and teachings of Muhammad.

In **Rahab: A Woman of Faith** (p. 28), we see Rahab the harlot, vulnerable because or her degrading occupation as prostitute but with high hopes for a better future, take the risk of hiding the Israelite spies, lying to the king about their whereabouts, and helping them escape. She represents all of the lower-class Canaanites who subverted their own highly stratified society in favor of the more just and egalitarian society of the invading Israelites, who promised to spare them and include them.

Drawing on participation in a local study group aligned with the Jesus Seminar in its quest for the historical Jesus, I portray **Jesus as a Non-Violent Resister** (p. 35) to the Roman Empire. Turning the left cheek, stripping naked in court, and walking a second mile are seen as gestures of guerrilla theater aiming to challenge Roman authority. Jesus is tried and executed by the Romans as a rival to Caesar.

Repentance (p. 45) pits Jesus against John the Baptist. John baptizes for forgiveness of sins. Jesus seeks baptism from John because he wants to be closer to God and is ready to take up his calling. John and Jesus both proclaim the kingdom of God. For John repentance means being penitent in fear of God's kingdom coming in judgment. For Jesus repentance means changing your mind and believing the good news of God's liberating kingdom at hand. John is austere. Jesus is convivial. John is like a punitive father. Jesus is like a nurturing mother. Therapy is most effective when conducted not in the framework of sin or sickness but in the framework of growth according to Virginia Satir.

Suggested by Valentine's Day and Ash Wednesday cropping up near each other, **Hearts and Ashes** (p. 51) presents three parallel schemes for how loves can be contrasted and combined. First there is red-hot passionate eros and mellow yellow storge mixed in orange self-giving agape in Alan John Lee's "Colors of Love." Second, in Freud there are the great forces of Love and Death, which can be joined in Communion. Third, there is seeker self and merger self which can unite in mutuality in Gail Sheehy's "Passages."   Finally a Latin chant affirms that where there is charitable love or romantic love, wherever there is love, there is God.

I call **Making Love Paramount** (p. 59) my kiss-of-death sermon because none of churches receiving it invited me to preach there again. In my home congregation, a woman walked out as soon as "sexuality" was mentioned. The framework was standard affirming the primacy of God's love, the greatest commands to love God and neighbor, and subordination of everything else to love. But the application was based on a report to the 1991 Presbyterian General Assembly on Sexuality, Spiritual, and Social Justice, which concluded that the real sin with homosexuality was not what gays, lesbians, and bisexuals do in their bedrooms out of love but the loveless way the church has treated them.

It's Okay to Be Gay: A Biblical Perspective (p. 67) examines in historical and literary context the six biblical passages that have been misused to clobber gays and points to a couple of positive examples such as David loving Jonathan more than women and Jesus healing the gay lover of a Roman centurion. The story of Sodom is dismissed as a tale of inhospitality and projected gang rape having nothing to do with gay love. In Romans 1 Paul sees same-sex sex as a symptom of idolatry, not as unnatural or wicked in its own right. Be prepared for lots of Greek terms!

In contrast with fundamentalists peddling cosmic life insurance in which the premium is accepting a certain set of beliefs and the reward is a heavenly life after death, **Being Saved by Being Lost** (p. 73) takes Jesus as a model embodying God's holy outreach as he gets down and dirty emptying himself and pouring himself out to save people from disease and oppression and saving them for a good abundant life. With the Protestant Reformation, salvation is seen as a free gift of grace not earned by works of Jewish law or Catholic ritual works or fundamentalist works of believing but gratefully expressed in justice and mercy and faith.

After a summer of training, a colleague and I worked with six congregations in northern California in the 1970s to help them understand and counteract their **White Racism** (p. 80). Here I share some basic insights, including discounting race as a symptom of racism, plus a couple of exercises that probe assumptions and stereotypes.

While working for a black Baptist church in inner city Cleveland in 1967, I met Martin Luther King and shook his hand when he helped us celebrate a victory of a grocery chain boycott aiming to have more Negroes hired and promoted. The closest I came to President Kennedy was watching a motorcade pass by my seminary in New York City in 1962, but I did write my PhD thesis about him. **Kennedy-King Dialogue** (p. 83) is my construction based on what they actually said to each other, public statements involving them, and plausible conversations. Here we have a confrontation between a prophetic preacher and a calculating politician. Under pressure from King and unfolding events we see Kennedy move from downplaying civil rights as an irritant to embracing the movement as a moral cause. The dialogue concludes with an epitaph for each figure after assassination. It is best read aloud by a pair of speakers and has been well received when so performed.

Martin Luther King as a Hero for Men (p. 90) portrays King as fulfilling the archetypal male roles of Warrior, Magician, Lover, and King (as recognized by the ManKind Project, to which I belong).

In 2009, I gave a **Speech on Just War** (p. 91) to an audience of pacifists, noting our differences but seeking cooperation. Drawn from ancient Greece and Rome and passing into Christianity by St. Augustine, criteria for a just war and laid out and applied to recent wars followed by President Obama's remarks while accepting the Nobel Peace Prize.

Also in 2009 I gave a **Speech on Gaza** (p. 97) condemning Israel's bombing of Gaza as unjust with the US implicated through aid to Israel.

A Vision of Peace (p. 99) envisages our disengaging from Iraq, resolving the Palestinian situation, getting at the roots of terrorism, and engaging in economic political, ecological, and religious reform.

In **An Ancient Heritage** (p. 101) I invite participants on an inter-generational retreat who are about to celebrate Communion to set aside conceptual thinking and open themselves up to primitive and archaic meanings of the sacrament as a symbolically powerful ritual enactment of killing and eating with echoes of animal, human, and divine sacrifice.

In a mock interview, best performed by a pair of people, I present **Spectator Sports as a Religion** (p. 108) seen in passionate devotion, primitive enthusiasm, team identification and symbols, school pride, and huge investment of time and money in stadiums and conversations.

Encapsulated in snippets from a couple of poems of mine, **Life Eternal** (p. 110) sees each of us in our span of life from birth to death enlivened and transformed by our participation in the eternal life and mission of God.

Thanks for joining me on a spree. You have been invited to construct your own religion from varied sources, to uphold religious pluralism in public prayer, to affirm the historic strands in Islam, to admire Rahab the harlot as a subversive, to follow Jesus as a non-violent resister to empire calling people to change their minds and believe the good news of God's liberating kingdom at hand, to experience multi-colored loves, to make love paramount with everything else subordinate, to convey that it is okay to be gay, to pour yourself out to save people from disease and oppression and to save them for a good abundant life as Jesus did, to acknowledge racism and fight for civil rights inspired by Martin Luther King as a hero, to protest wars that are unjust, to seek peace, to savor the primitive aspects of Communion, to note spectator sports as a religion, and to celebrate our mortal life related to God's eternal life.

Making Peace Among Religions Within Myself

In looking at the wide sweep of history
in "Religion in the Making," Alfred North Whitehead
says that religion has probably done more harm than good.
I would agree.
As my atheist friends remind me (as if I were responsible)
there have been more than enough of crusades, holy wars,
pogroms, massacres, despotisms, spats, bigotry, abuse.
But what if we combined the best of each religion?
That's what I have done.
I did not set out to do it,
but that is what happened.

If I can make peace among religions within myself,
then maybe this can be a basis
for making peace among religions in the world.
If I am Jewish myself, how can I be mean to Jews?
If I a Muslim, won't I be in a position to understand
both mainstream Islam and the radical Islamists?

The conventional approach to religions is to see them
as systems of belief which contradict each other
so that you would have to choose one over another
with the proof of who is right coming in an afterlife.
This is way off base in my view.

Personally, I do not believe in an afterlife
so we will never know who is right
if that is the name of the game.
I believe in eternal life, which is life with the eternal.
When my life is over, life itself continues.
And I don't think religions are just systems of belief.
When we teach religious studies at IUPUI,
we recognize seven dimensions in religions,
not just the doctrinal dimension but also experiential,
ritual, mythological, aesthetic, ethical, and social.

Religions and persons differ
in the emphasis they put on various dimensions.
Judaism is more a set of practices than of beliefs.
Right belief is an early stage on the Eightfold Path
to enlightenment in Buddhism.
Episcopalians center on prayer and sacraments.
It was said of Santayana that he believed "there is no God,
and Mary is his mother"; theology left him cold,
but he had a warm spot in his heart for Marian piety.

My own approach is to interweave seven religions
into a beautiful tapestry rich in many dimensions:
resonating with the fulminations of the Hebrew prophets,
following Jesus as a non-violent resister to empire,
enjoying delightfully quirky zen Buddhist stories,
finding excellent insights in the poems of the Tao te Ching
admiring the charitableness of Muslims,
experiencing nature's enchantments as in ancient religions,
thinking freely in a modern and skeptical vein,
being always open to fresh ideas as I dialogue with others.

Much of this is expressed in my book, "A Song of Faith,"
which tells my story and sings my faith,
shares my poems and expounds science poetically,
recounts developmental stages for humanity and individuals.
It takes off from a remark by Episcopal Bishop James Pike:
he does not believe the creed when said but only when sung.
It ends with a statement of my credo:

My motto is: Why have one religion when you can have
several? From my Jewish faith, I derive a commitment to
justice and to "tikkun olam" (repairing the world). From
my Christian faith, I add love and forgiveness. From my
Buddhist faith, I generate compassion and paying attention.
From my Taoist faith, I practice inner peace and flexible
strength. From my Muslim faith, I draw kindness and
concern for the poor. From my Wiccan faith, I recover
closeness to nature and protection for Mother Earth. From
my Humanist faith, I venture into freedom of thought and
building a human community. I celebrate this religious
diversity within myself and among us.

Let us begin with the end: with freedom of thought.
I was a skeptical philosopher long before I was a believer,
and I do my believing in a way that some may think unusual.
Along with Paul Tillich in "Dynamics of Faith,
I make a huge distinction between faith and belief.
Faith is an attitude of trust and confidence;
belief is assent to statements.
I have changed my beliefs a lot without undoing my faith.
And I don't see religious beliefs as descriptive truths.
Linguistic analyst philosophers tell us religious language
gains power because it is peculiar, not conveying
information but sparking insight and revelation.
My approach can be called "symbolic realism."
Names for the divine, scriptures, bread & wine are symbols
that do not capture the divine but point to divine reality.
Many symbols, many stories, many poems can illuminate.

Humanism frames my combining religions together.
Religions are human enterprises
and at their finest seek to create the finest humanity.
Ludwig Feuerbach claimed that God is a projection
of the best of humanity, which is worthy of our worship.
To a large extent, I concur.

Our humanism goes all the way back to the ancient Greeks
with Protagoras saying "man is the measure of all things"
as Socrates says "the unexamined life is not worth living."
From the Greeks we get our basic ethics: classical virtues
of justice, wisdom, courage, and moderation.
Greeks glorify war too much for my tastes, but I've heard
that the just war theory I use came originally from them.
Open dialogue about ideas that matter as a basis
for human community is a legacy of ancient Greece,
and though our science has progressed immensely since then,
the Greeks pioneered a skeptical and scientific attitude.

Science is very good in its field, but there is no need
for a scientism, which tries to monopolize truth.
There is no reason we cannot combine modern science and
ancient wisdom, or wicca, solving problems masterfully and
apprehending mystery wonderfully.

The earliest people we know about,
as represented by today's Bushmen in the Kalahari desert,
were gentle and egalitarian.
War had not yet been invented,
and older children taught younger ones to resolve conflict.
When an antelope was killed and brought back to the clan,
everyone got a relatively equal portion to eat.
When the antelope and tubers in an area thinned,
the nomadic clansmen would move on, and nature recovered.

American Indians were a little more developed,
but they continued to identify with natural elements,
seeing the same water in the rivers coursing through them
and respecting earth as their mother.

I like to commune with nature and to befriend my pets.
On Mankind Project gatherings,
we live in the woods and call in the seven directions
and have sweat lodges based on Indian models.
Taking part in the environment movements also pits me
on the side of taking care of our abused, warming planet.
Being close to nature and protecting mother earth
is part of my religion.

Further development led to settled agriculture
and a food surplus, which was a boon to mankind,
but the way it was handled turned it into a wrong turn
as it led to inequality and domination by kings and nobles
and morphed into brutal, war-glorifying empire.

In China, one of the four cradles of civilization,
Confucianism reinforced a system of subordinations:
son to father, younger brother to older, wife to husband,
youngsters to elders, and all subjects to the emperor.
Taoism repudiates artificial society to copy nature.

The Tao is the source of all that is.
Everything comes from it and returns to it.
It is an unnamable mystery no one can pinpoint,
yet prolific in its progeny.
It accomplishes great things
but does not seek recognition.
The tao is like a river running to the sea naturally.

The man of tao acts as if not acting, effortlessly.
He does not compete or contend. No fight: no blame.
He goes through life like an empty boat;
if someone collides with him, there is no one to curse.
He does not puff himself up.
If someone can burst your bubble,
you must have been inflated.
The man of tao takes from the rich and gives to the poor;
he knows when enough is enough and leads from behind,
not seeking to force and control but to model and inspire.
He empties his mind of desires and thoughts and ambitions
and thus finds inner peace.
I humbly polish my mirror
so those who meet me do not see me
but see themselves in my light.

As my spiritual discipline coming out of Warrior Monk,
I read a poem a day from the "Tao te Ching,"
a collection of 81 poems from around 500 BC,
and since then I have been collecting translations
and currently am examining the Chinese words.

The hero of the "Tao te Ching" is water.
Water is the weakest thing in the world;
when you step in water it steps aside.
Yet water penetrates rocks, freezes, breaks them apart.
The rigid branch breaks in the wind; the flexible bends.
The man of tao finds strength in apparent weakness.

People sometimes ask me why I do not include Hinduism,
especially since I am a great admirer of Mahatma Gandhi.
The main reason is because Hinduism is not a religion
but a collection of religions. Near the Indus river,
the land is India, language is Hindi, religion Hinduism.
but these outsider terms mask much diversity.
Most Indians are caste-bound archaic polytheists
though a few engage in yogas of deeds or devotion.
The Hindu way of knowledge is similar enough to Buddhism
that I can conflate the two.

Gautama Siddhartha is called Buddha, the Enlightened One.
Contrary to the Hindu endorsement of ordinary life
with mystical religion as a supplement late in life,
the Buddha abandoned family and job in a quest for insight
and organized followers as world-renouncing monks and nuns.
Buddha taught that 1) life is suffering, 2) the source of
suffering is craving, and 3) the solution is non-striving,
and he laid out an Eightfold Path running from right
attitude and belief to right mindfulness and meditation.
When we refuse to accept life with its limitations,
when we cling to each other, when we seek to get ahead,
when we try to shore ourselves up by accumulating things,
we increase our suffering.
When we embrace death and illness and loss and simplicity
and live in the present and pay attention to what happens,
stopping to smell the roses,
life blossoms before our eyes.
Giving up the illusion of a separated self,
We realize that we are connected to everything that is
and feel compassion for all living beings.

Buddhism and Taoism combine in Zen Buddhism,
which is my favorite form of Buddhism.
Every once in a while I visit a Zen Buddhist sangha
featuring a half hour of seated meditation
and a half hour of walking meditation plus conversation.
I especially like zen buddhist stories, collected in "101
Zen Stories" on-line & in Paul Reps' "Zen Flesh, Zen Bones"
There is a story of the professor so full of his knowledge
that he has no room in his cup for further learning.
There is a monk who carries a woman over a stream and sets
her down while the monk who complains is still carrying her
There is the nun who funnels incense smoke so others cannot
have it and blackens the nose of her Buddha statue.
There is a zen master, hearing what Jesus says about not
worrying but trusting like birds and lilies of the field,
remarking that the one speaking is not far from buddhahood.

Judaism, Christianity, and Islam belong to a western stream
of religions, which see the divine active in human history.
God reveals his name to Moses as Yahweh,
the one who makes to be what comes to pass.
Yahweh leads his people from slavery in imperial Egypt
to freedom in a land of promise
by way of slogging through the sea of reeds
and wandering for years in the desert
giving them a Law to live by en route, a second gift.
And God continues to liberate those who are oppressed:
from America's black slaves to downtrodden labor movements
to those aversely affected by American imperial policies,
God using us radicals as instruments of his will.

The ancient Hebrews were more egalitarian than most,
and their infiltration of Canaan was welcomed
by lower-class Canaanites, such as Rahab the Harlot,
who helped to overthrow their Canaanite overlords.
Yet being in charge of their lives within the bounds of Law
was seen as not enough as Hebrews hankered for greatness
asking to have a kingship established like the nations
though prophets warn that they will be worse off when
their sons are soldiers and daughters cook for the court.

Prophets confronted kings who broke God's Law
and excoriated the rich for trampling the poor.
They contended that God was not hoodwinked by ritual piety.
"Take away from me the noise of your solemn assemblies.
To the melodies of your harps I will not listen," says God.
"But let justice roll down like waters,
And righteousness like a mighty stream," Amos exclaims.

Destruction of kingdoms of Israel and Judah a century apart
followed by exile abroad saddened and chastened the Jews,
who hung up their harps and wept when they thought of Zion,
who saw themselves as Yahweh's suffering servant,
whose patient bearing of abuse was redemptive,
who rejoiced when some returned to Judea.
"Comfort ye, comfort ye, my people," says your God.
"Speak ye comfortably to Jerusalem, that
her warfare is accomplished and her iniquity is pardoned."
The experience of exile led to hopes for a messianic age
when peace would prevail and law would be written on hearts
led not by tyrants but a prince meek & lowly riding an ass.
They broadened their idea of God from a God of one people
to God of all nations and creator of the universe,
who relied on people to join him in making the world
better.

Jesus of Nazareth is called Christ, the Anointed One.
Jesus saw himself as anointed by the Spirit of Yahweh
to bring good news to the poor, sight to the blind,
freedom for prisoners, and announcement of the Jubilee year
when debts would be canceled and ancestral lands returned.
Tribute to Caesar, taxes to Herod, and tithes to the Temple
would often take away two thirds of a peasant's harvest
forcing him into debt, foreclosure, and imprisonment.

In line with the Hebrew prophets,
Jesus elevated justice and mercy and faith
over keeping laws on tithing, eating kosher, and Sabbath.
Those showing the inbreaking kingdom of God fed the hungry,
clothed the naked, ministered to the sick and prisoners.
Jesus would heal anyone, including lepers and the gay lover
of a Roman centurion, anytime, including the Sabbath.
Jesus ate and drank with toll collectors and whores,
whom he found more open to God's way than the religious.
When a woman of the streets anointed Jesus' head and feet,
he said she was forgiven much because she loved much.
Jesus called people to be all-inclusive as God is,
who blesses everyone, just or unjust, with sun and rain.
He called on his followers to love even their enemies.

Jesus elevated Jewish commandments to love God and neighbor
to pre-eminence subordinating all else to these invitations
When challenged to illustrate love for neighbor,
he told the story of a despised Samaritan who ministered
to a man beaten up by thieves while others passed him by.
Jesus was a non-violent resister to the Roman Empire.
If a superior gives your right cheek a humiliating backslap
he recommends defying him by turning your other cheek,
which he cannot slap with his (only available) right hand.
If a creditor takes your coat in court as payment for debt,
give him your underwear to shame him for his naked greed.
If a Roman soldier makes you carry his pack for one mile,
get him into trouble by carrying it illegally for two miles
When followers tried to land the top spots, Jesus said
"Gentiles lord it over one another, but we do not;
whoever is greatest is servant of all."
Jesus did not want to dominate, being called "Lord, Lord,"
but saw those who respond to God as belonging to God's folk

Jesus was executed by the Romans as a rival to Caesar.
To a father who forgives his prodigal son, Jesus prayed,
"Father, forgive them for they know not what they do."
Love and forgiveness is what I value as a follower of
Jesus.

Muhammad did not seek to proclaim a new god,
but to bring the God of Jews and Christians to the Arabs.
He called God Al-Lah, the God, the one and only God.
Islam means submission to God, and a Muslim is a submitter
(though as a muslim I see myself cooperating with God).
Islam is a simple religion, summarized in its five pillars.
The first pillar is belief that there is no God but Allah
and that Muhammad is his spokesperson.
The second pillar is public prayer five times a day.
The third pillar is zakat, charity for the poor.
The fourth pillar is fasting and feasting during Ramadan.
The fifth is the hajj, the recommended pilgrimage to Mecca.

I am most impressed with Islam seeing God as benevolent
and requiring us be kind as well.
Many religions talk about being good to the poor
but find ways to avoid living it out.
Christians quote Jesus, "the poor are always with you"
without its sequel "do good to them whenever you can."
In some muslim countries zakat is a tax of 2.5% on wealth;
fasting in Ramadan is seen as sharing privations of poor,
who are invited to take part in feasting at day's end.

Although some twisted forms of Islam today are intolerant,
it was quite the opposite in the original Islam of Muhammad
He said there was no need to convert "people of the book,"
Jews and Christians who believe in the same God as Muslims.
Islam honors all of the prophets, especially major prophets
Abraham, Moses, Jesus, and Muhammad.
There is a book in the Qur'an devoted to Jesus' mother.
One of Muhammad's uncles was a Christian,
and several Jewish tribes were part of the ummah,
the political community which Muhammad headed.
One Jewish tribe betrayed him and sided with his enemies.
It was exterminated for treason, not because of religion;
the other loyal Jewish tribes remained quite accepted.

We end where we began with building a human community,
this time as an umma which encompasses several religions
and seeks to build a just and benevolent society.
It is not only a community of freedom of thought & dialogue
but also a community of closeness to nature & mother earth,
peace and pliability, compassion and attention, justice and
effort, love and forgiveness, kindness and charitableness.

I take on and invite you to be an interfaith activist, who
combines insights and practices from several religions in
order to accept and make a good self, relations and world.

A Town Called Greece

The town of Greece, NY moved from rotating prayer-giving among Christian congregations only to inviting a Jewish layman and the chairman of the local Baha'i temple to deliver prayers and allowing a Wiccan priestess who had read press reports about the prayer controversy to give the invocation at the monthly meeting of the Greece Town Council. We will examine the constitutionality of this practice, the interaction of ecclesiastical and civil religion, the content of prayers allowed and preferred, and the spirit of pluralism hopefully evoked.

In "Town of Greece v. Galloway" the US Supreme Court affirmed the constitutionality of such prayers: "That the First Congress provided for the appointment of chaplains only days after approving language for the First Amendment demonstrates that the Framers considered legislative prayer a benign acknowledgment of religion's role in society."

I recognize two kinds of religion, ecclesiastical and civil. Ecclesiastical religion emanates from churches, synagogues, mosques, sanghas, etc. Civil religion focuses on the whole society. The earliest religions were civil. Australian aborigines directed their devotion to the clan to the totem that stood for the clan. Americans direct their devotion to country to the flag in the Pledge of Allegiance to the Flag: "I pledge allegiance to the flag of the United States of America and to the republic for which it stands, one nation, under God, indivisible, with liberty and justice for all." Although the phrase "under God," added in the 1950s, is the most explicitly civil religious, the whole pledge was already religious. The flag is so sacred that mistreating it is regarded as desecrating it. The common sacred values of liberty and justice for all are affirmed.

You can see plenty of American civil religion on the back of the dollar bill. The national motto is there: "In God We Trust." The eye of God is pictured over the pyramid with the caption "Annuit Coeptis;" He [God] oversees our undertakings. Under the pyramid is the caption "Novus Ordo Seclorum:" the new order of the ages, which began on the date recorded in the base of the pyramid in Roman numerals MDCCLXXVI (1776), when the United States declared its independence. Presidential proclamations are doubly dated: in the year of our Lord 2014 A.D. (Anno Domini) and in the year of these United States 238, implying that there are two centers to history: the birth of Jesus and the birth of America.

I define civil religion as "Devotion to a nation and its leaders, its ideals and gods expressed in words such as speeches, songs, and documents and in deeds such as ceremonies, wars, and monuments." American civil religion tends to be rather generic. It tends to speak of God in very general terms rather than mentioning Jesus or Muhammad or Moses or Buddha. For instance, reflecting the deism of the Founding Fathers, the Declaration of Independence posits the right to revolution as based on the laws of Nature and of Nature's God and rights to life, liberty, and pursuit of happiness as endowed by the Creator.

In terms of amounts of ecclesiastical religion (which is "sectarian" in Court lingo) and civil (civic) religion, what kind of prayer would be good to offer? Respondents Susan Galloway and Linda Stephens objected that the prayers violated their religious or philosophical views with Galloway admonishing board members that she found the prayers "offensive," "intolerable," and an affront to a "diverse community." Justice Kagan in her dissent quotes a prayer that she sees as much too "sectarian:"

"The beauties of spring . . . are an expressive symbol of the new life of the risen Christ. The Holy Spirit was sent to the apostles at Pentecost so that they would be courageous witnesses of the Good News to different regions of the Mediterranean world and beyond. The Holy Spirit continues to be the inspiration and the source of strength and virtue, which we all need in the world of today. And so . . . [w]e pray this evening for the guidance of the Holy Spirit as the Greece Town Board meets."

Much less sectarian and seemingly more appropriate is the invocation given by the Rev. Richard Barbour at the September 2006 board meeting:

"Gracious God, you have richly blessed our nation and this community. Help us to remember your generosity and give thanks for your goodness. Bless the elected leaders of the Greece Town Board as they conduct the business of our town this evening. Give them wisdom, courage, discernment and a single-minded desire to serve the common good. We ask your blessing on all public servants, and especially on our police force, firefighters, and emergency medical personnel. . . . Respectful of every religious tradition, I offer this prayer in the name of God's only son Jesus Christ, the Lord, Amen."

Ironically, ecclesiastical content, at which some take offense, cannot be ruled out in favor of civil religion alone. According to the majority opinion:

> Respondents argue, in effect, that legislative prayer may be addressed only to a generic God. The law and the Court could not draw this line for each specific prayer or seek to require ministers to set aside their nuanced and deeply personal beliefs for vague and artificial ones. . . Government may not mandate a civic religion that stifles any but the most generic reference to the sacred any more than it may prescribe a religious orthodoxy. . .
> To hold that invocations must be nonsectarian would force the legislatures that sponsor prayers and the courts that are asked to decide these cases to act as supervisors and censors of religious speech, a rule that would involve government in religious matters to a far greater degree than is the case under the town's current practice of neither editing or approving prayers in advance nor criticizing their content after the fact. . . The suggestion that government may establish an official or civic religion as a means of avoiding the establishment of a religion with more specific creeds strikes us as a contradiction that cannot be accepted. Once it invites prayer into the public sphere, government must permit a prayer-giver to address his or her own God or gods as conscience dictates, unfettered by what an administrator or judge considers to be nonsectarian.

The majority opinion sees prayers as not only permissible but desirable in a pluralistic context:

> From the Nation's earliest days, invocations have been addressed to assemblies comprising many different creeds, striving for the idea that people of many faiths may be united in a community of tolerance and devotion, even if they disagree as to religious doctrine. The prayers delivered in Greece do not fall outside this tradition. They may have invoked, e.g., the name of Jesus, but they also invoked universal themes, e.g., by calling for a spirit of cooperation. This tradition permits chaplains to ask their own God for blessings of peace, justice, and freedom that find appreciation among people of all faiths. That a prayer is given in the name of Jesus, Allah, or Jehovah, or that it makes passing reference to religious doctrines, does not remove it from that tradition.

Finally, the majority opinion sees religious themes as providing particular means to universal ends.

> Prayer that reflects beliefs specific to only some creeds can still serve to solemnize the occasion, so long as the practice over time is not exploited to proselytize or advance any one, or to disparage any other, faith or belief. Prayers offered to Congress often seek peace for the Nation, wisdom for its lawmakers, and justice for its people, values that count as universal and are embodied not only in religious traditions, but in our founding documents and laws.

Pluralism is what the Court's majority opinion favored and found in Greece, and pluralism is what the dissenting opinions wanted more of. The majority were impressed with the broader range of prayers in Greece while dissenters claim that Greece reverted to the prior pattern of rotation once the period of Court scrutiny was over. Recognizing that "we are a cosmopolitan nation made up of people of almost every conceivable religious preference," Justice Kagan in her dissent indicates a readiness to welcome the opportunity to involve people from various ecclesiastical persuasions in public prayer. The upshot of "Town of Greece v. Galloway" is affirmation of the unity in plurality of religions treated equally in public, just as the dollar bill proclaims: *E pluribus unum*, out of many one.

Modernism and Islam

My chief academic contribution has been the development of a set of ideal types of religion: archaic, historic, and modern. An ideal type is an extreme conceptual model used to analyze actual situations. It is my contention that the type of religion is more significant than the brand (e.g., Islam, Christianity) and a key to sorting out good religion and bad. The nub of the distinction between types is that archaic religion deifies society, historic religion deifies a transcendent God, and modern religion deifies the self.

Modern religion (or "modernism" as an alternative to religion) elevates egotism, secularism, and scientific rationalism.

Modernism rests upon egotism. Ultimate authority in the ideology of Locke and Jefferson resides in individuals who compact together to form society and government in order to protect their rights without interfering with their freedom. Secularization and rationalization erode commitments to overarching values so that anything besides the pursuit of individual self-interest is regarded--by economists--as irrational. The result, according to Max Weber, is "specialists without spirit, sensualists without heart." The divine is either dismissed or localized in autonomous individual selves who acknowledge no authority higher than the laws their own representatives have framed.

Modernism promotes secularism. It has no problem with religion as long as it remains a private matter. Individuals have the right to pursue their spiritual concerns in any way they want, but religion has no place in the public square.

Modernism espouses scientific rationalism. Whatever cannot be proved rationally, i.e., scientifically, is supercritically dismissed. Myths and doctrines are seen as mere fabrications, taken literally rather than symbolically, and then rejected as such. Past forms of order make no claims on the present. You may do what you wish as long you do no harm to others. Tradition is of no value, and innovation is the rule.

Because the fundamentalism underlying al-Qaida ideology comes mainly from Egypt, we will focus on modernization there, to which it responds.

After 1800, a young Albanian army officer, Muhammad Ali, took over Egypt. He made himself personal owner of every acre of land in the country, took over religiously endowed lands, achieved a monopoly of every trade and industrial enterprise, encouraged European trade to penetrate Egypt and destroyed the indigenous merchant class. The Islamic leadership (ulema) lost their traditional tax-exempt status, were marginalized and starved financially, their Qu'ran schools in ruins; they became reactionary. A modern state was achieved not by innovation (as in Europe) but by imitation of the West: not empowerment, autonomy, and innovation but deprivation, dependence, and patchy, imperfect imitation. Military officers got a western education; the people did not even get primary education.

Nasser in the 1960s called for a cultural revolution in the name of "scientific socialism." He outlawed the Muslim Brotherhood, which was largely an educational and social-service organization though it had a tiny terrorist wing. Religion was seen as responsible for the "false consciousness" that held the Arabs back. Islamic leader Sayyid Qtub (before he became a fundamentalist) said of American culture: "Any objectives other than the immediate utilitarian ones are by-passed, and any human element other than ego is not recognized. While the whole of life is dominated by such materialism, there is no scope for laws beyond provisions for labor and production."

In 1972, Sadat attempted to bring Egypt into the capitalist world market. This benefited a small percentage of the rising bourgeoisie, but the vast majority suffered. The ostentatious consumerism of the elite aroused intense disgust and discontent. The young especially felt alienated. Only about 4% of them could expect a decent job. Many were forced to leave home and work in wealthy oil states. A lady's maid in a foreign household in Egypt was likely to earn more than an assistant university professor. Universities were so overcrowded, one could not hear the professor; learning was by rote and did not lead to jobs. In 1978, Sadat's Law of Shame outlawed any criticism of his regime. He broke ranks with the Arab world by making peace with Israel. In 1981, he was assassinated. No Arab leader attended his funeral, and no crowds mourned him.

Archaic Religion and Islam

Archaic religion features idolatry, repression, and literalism.

Archaic religion rests upon idolatry. It divinizes some social entity: society, state, church or book ("Bibliolatry" has been coined to mean idolizing Bible, Quran, or some other book). The sacred object of devotion has absolute authority and must be obeyed without question.

Archaic religion promotes repression. It stresses order, and it fears freedom as an invitation to chaos. It has a firm knowledge of good and evil and avoids the search for true goodness out of self-righteousness. Evil is seen as external to the divine state or church or ummah, which, In all innocence, opposes its demonic enemies. It pursues holy war gauged to force complete surrender. Factionalism, partisanship, and dissent are disparaged as disloyal and crushed as a threat to heteronomous rule; church and state are not at odds but in cahoots.

Archaic religion espouses literalism. Experience outshines reason, and *mythos* dwarfs *logos*; reigning tradition brooks no innovation. A golden age in the past is glorified over against the present. Human nature Is regarded as basically evil and unchanging, requiring the continued application of time-test traditional sanctions to tame man.

The earliest religions came close to the archaic type from the mild form in primitive societies to the repressive ancient empires. When people try to go back to the archaic, they can never return to what it was because their options are different. Fundamentalism is a form of archaism drummed up to withstand modernism, and it is very selective and innovative in the way it uses tradition. Like creedalism, which puts stress on what is under dispute rather than what is central, it places importance in what previous believers would have found tangential. It cannot be naïve and unscientific in it literalism, as ancients would be, but its literalism takes on an anti-scientific flavor, and the pacific strains in its heritage are drowned out by a militant siege mentality.

Where justification by faith has already been perverted into salvation by belief in "conservative" Protestantism, fundamentalism stresses literalism. In Catholicism sacraments are central and safely sacrosanct, and past popes used their claimed infallibility to further Mariolatry.

In response to Nasser's attempt to sideline Islam in Egypt and his suppression of the Muslim Brotherhood, Sayyid Qtub arose as the "founder of Sunni fundamentalism." He was greatly influenced by the writings of Abul Ala Mawdudi, a Pakistani journalist and politician, who sounds somewhat historic in his emphasis on the sovereignty of God, but who took it in an archaic direction in espousing totalitarian rule with no room for human innovation. Mawdudi paralleled the godlessness of modern westernization to the barbarism that Muhammad confronted in pre-Islamic Arabia, and he was the first to turn jihad, which simply means "struggle," into a universal holy war against modernization and to make it a central tenet of Islam. Arrested and executed as a member of the Muslim Brotherhood, Qtub drew this jihad into four stages paralleling what Muhammad did: 1) forming a vanguard apart from the godless; 2) making a complete rupture with society like Muhammad's migration (hijrah) to Medina; 3) establishing an Islamic state; 4) armed struggle against un believers like Muhammad taking Mecca.

Anwar Sadat released surviving Muslim Brothers from prison and allowed them to publish a monthly journal, which routinely denounced the enemies of Islam. Shukri Mastafa, who had been in Nasser's camps and was executed for the murder of a scholar who called him a heretic, founded the Society of Muslims, which excommunicated all of Egypt's religious and political leaders as pagans and encouraged migration to poor neighborhoods to protest the wealth of the elite. The press called them Takfir wal Hijrah (Excommunication & Migration). The Islamic Group (Jamaat al-Islamiyyah) worked to create Islamic zones on university campuses, fostered Islamic dress and segregation of the sexes in lecture halls, stressed migration from mainstream society, and attacked cinemas, Egyptian Christians, and tourists.

Many turned to the secret cells of Jihad, founded by physician Ayman al-Zawahiri, who shaped the mind of bin Laden. Jihad put a narrow stress On the Verses of the Sword in the Qu'ran, where Muslims are told to "slay those who ascribe divinity to aught beside God," which was seen to include the outwardly Musllim Sadat because he, like the Mongol rulers, was an "apostate" who ruled by laws other than the Sharia. Khaled Islamabouli, a Jihadist, assassinated Sadat in 1981 calling him infidel and Pharaoh. Zawahiri was imprisoned for three years, was cut from leadership in Jihad when he rejected its cease-fire (after Luxor killings). and joined the struggle against the Soviets in Afghanistan as a medic.

9/11: Behind the Veil

The atrocious attack on the World Trade Center and the Pentagon has left many Americans groping for an explanation. People ask, "How can anyone hate us so much that they would take innocent lives in such a wholesale fashion? What did we ever do to them?" Well, plenty. As the world's sole military superpower and center of world capitalism, the U.S. leads the world.

Muslim fundamentalism has long been critical of modernity. Ayatollah Khomeini reversed the modernization of Iran as an affront to Islamic values and excoriated the U.S. as the Great Satan because it led the modern West. Modern democracy deifies the individual who can, in concert, enact and repeal any laws he pleases irrespective of tradition. Modern capitalism enshrines individual self-interest as the highest value and expects corporations to maximize profits at any cost. Those who tried to bomb the World Trade Center in 1993 sought to topple "the towers that constitute the pillars of their civilization."

Discontent fuels lashing out at America, the West, and modern civilization. Palestinians have lived under Israeli occupation or in refugee camps for many years at a subsistence level while Jewish settlements encroach and hog scarce water. Afghanistan has an average per capita annual income of $800. Dissidents are prone to rise up against their perceived persecutors not in strength but in the impotence of "terrorism," which is what those in power call the lawless acts of those denied power. A child throws a rock at a soldier. A suicide pilot, inspired by the militant Islamic fundamentalism of al-Zawahiri and al Qaida, rams a tower. Envying us because we are rich or demonizing us because we are godless, it is David taking out Goliath with a slingshot, the pious overcoming the philistine. Rubbing out Osama bin Laden as the mastermind behind the plane rammings has created another martyr and may increase resentment and lead to more terror.

Muslim militants cannot succeed in stemming the ruthless onslaught of modern capitalism, but it is ours to harness and temper. There is something between the archaism of the fundamentalists and modern individualism, something I call "historic" religion. It appeals to a transcendent God, to ideals beyond money-making, to community, to the common good; it depends on conscience, not coercion. We saw it in response to 9/11: in the heroism of rescue workers who laid aside their self-interest to help, in world political and religious leaders calling for justice and tolerance, in a President's prayer for God's guidance. More of it would do us a world of good.

Historic Islam

Historic religion fosters transcendence, self-control, and symbolism.

Historic religion aspires to transcendence. It affirms itself only as an imperfect vehicle for seeking to be faithful to the divine beyond it. Apprehension of the sacred is mediated through concrete but ambiguous experience. Not only can God's action in human history be seen in the past or anticipated in the future, but ordinary moments of the present can be transparent to the divine. Bearing God's image, every human is freely responsible to carry out God's loving will as discerned by conscience.

Historic religion encourages self-control. Within the divine order, people may freely experiment with their institutions. Historic religion is not comfortable with either an absolutized morality or a privatized one. Recognizing a limited knowledge of good and evil, it sees good and evil mixed ambivalently in varying proportions in all persons and nations, and it is willing to make proximate judgments to that effect. The search for true goodness is a public and dialogical quest resulting in a pursuit of compromised values, which seeks to transform current realities in the light of transcendent ideals and in the power of immanent divinity. Deliberate choice of the lesser evil is often the best a person or a nation can do. This may justify a war as a last and temporary resort within the broader pursuit of peace as a reconciliation of conflict, as an organic assembly of humankind, and as a divine gift of harmony. Rather than advocating complete self-sacrifice for nation or complete self-indulgence, it seeks to balance the claims of nation and self in faithfulness to God.

Historic religion feeds on symbolism. Myths and doctrines are conceded to be human constructions reflecting the time, place, and thought forms of their origin, but such myths and doctrines are felt to be compelling rather than arbitrary and are seen as essential stimulants to treasured perspectives and commitments. Tradition is both maintained and revised gradually. Historic belief is self-critical, able to see its own shortcomings, ready to challenge the deification of its own formulations when they cease to point symbolically beyond themselves. Historic religion seeks a whole person whose unconscious feelings and conscious thoughts are in dialogue with each other, who balances his being and his doing, who is able to speak the whole range of human languages from archetypes to concepts, being neither a stranger to his own depths nor one who finds mundane life profane.

Along with the emergence of Taoism, Buddhism, & Platonism in the first millennium B.C., a quest for transcendence was expressed in the rise of monotheistic religions in the Near East--starting with Judaism, continuing with Christianity, and culminating in Islam. The religions of the Semites feature a transcendent God whose first good gift is deliverance and whose second good gift is law. Hebrew religion features Moses, the prototypical Prophet (nabi) who speaks God's word, and David, the model Prince (messiah), who, despites lapses, rules with justice. Christianity features Jesus, who is God's word made flesh and a messiah (christ) who redeems as he fails. Islam features Muhammad, who is Prophet and leader.

Islam means surrender and promises the peace (salaam) that surrender yields. Muhammad submitted to God (al-Lah) in receiving the revelations that he then recited (quran) and in following the divine mandate for justice, equity, and compassion. Prostration in prayer punctuating each day expressed submission to a great and merciful God and the setting aside of pride and selfishness as did giving alms to the poor and sharing the privations of the poor in a month of fasting. Like Jesus, Muhammad was rejected by the leaders of his hometown Mecca. The muslim ethic of sharing flew in the face of the new emerging cut-throat capitalism of Mecca. After Muhammad's clan was boycotted and starved, he accepted the invitation to make a migration (hijrah) to Yathrib, which became a model City (Medina) after Muhammad subdued its warring tribes into a single non-violent muslim community (ummah). The muslims and Meccans fought several battles, but Muhammad made a gesture of peace when he went to Mecca on pilgrimage (hajj), a haven of non-violence where people of all races and religions gather as equals to express submission to the divine. After a peace treaty was made and violated, Muhammed marched on Mecca with ten thousand troops; the city fell without bloodshed.

Archaic Islam ossifies the revelations, laws, and structures of the formative period, and archaic fundamentalism sees migration as repudiation of society and struggle against enemies as key. Historic Islam applies principles forged in its origins to developing understandings and arrangements and works on reform of society through the largely non-violent struggle that Muhammad favored. Its sense of a community of sharing inspires cooperation mitigating the selfishness of modern individualistic capitalism, and its stress on consultation (shurah) in decision-making instigates a replacement of authoritarian regimes with a democracy of conscience.

Rahab: A Woman of Faith (Joshua 2:1-14, Matt. 1:1-16, Hebrews 11:29-12:2)

This morning we are going to examine a woman of faith, a rather unusual woman by our conventional standards. Her name is Rahab the harlot, a prostitute. Has it ever struck you as odd to find a prostitute listed in the Bible among the heroes of faith? Me too. Prostitution was regarded as a degrading occupation in biblical times just as in our own. As it turns out, however, being degraded is a significant ingredient in Rahab's becoming a woman of faith, and in the topsy-turvy world of biblical values this woman, whom it would be so easy to despise, receives nothing but praise. The Bible presents Rahab as a woman of faith—in her hope, her vulnerability, and her action.

HOPE

It is a distinctive characteristic of the book of Hebrews to portray faith as hope, hope in the fulfillment of the promises of God. This is a rather different view from that of St. Paul, who regards faith as trust in God's forgiveness and rather similar to that of the author of Revelation, who regards faith as hopeful fidelity to God in the midst of persecution. Generally, St. Paul's view of faith has ruled the day. The book of Hebrews is hobbled by a dualistic worldview and arcane priestly analogies while the book of Revelation is full of wild visions and occasional vindictiveness; both books barely made the canon of scripture. And yet both books contain some sterling passages. One of these, in my opinion, is the eleventh chapter of Hebrews, an almost lyrical song to the heroes and heroines of faith as hope, which I think needs to be taken seriously as an alternative to the Pauline view of faith. This chapter begins with a definition of faith: "Faith is the substance of things hoped for, the conviction of things not seen." The whole chapter's illustrations portray faith as hope, as confidence in a God who will fulfill his promises and bring into being a world more full of his presence and goodness than the world we now know. Even God shows faith in his own creativity when he creates the universe out of nothing, bringing into being things which had not been.

The author of Hebrews catalogues the human heroes of faith, among whom Rahab is numbered, the only woman named in the list. Then he notes the suffering which unnamed people of faith underwent in faithfulness to the promises of God which were not fulfilled in their day. Surrounded by such a cloud of witnesses and martyrs, much more should we who live in the era of the fulfillment of promise in Christ persevere in faith and hope following Jesus the pioneer and perfecter of our faith, the author of Hebrews admonishes us.

Rahab the harlot exhibits faith as hope by sticking out her neck and taking a gamble. Hers was the third of a series of three gambles that the book of Joshua mentions. The Israelites took a gamble when they crossed the sea of reeds—here erroneously called the Red Sea—trusting that God would provide them with a way through it while the Egyptians in hot pursuit would be hopelessly mired in it. The men of Israel took a big gamble when they attacked, as they occasionally did, the seemingly impregnable fortified cities of Canaan. More often the Israelites took over the Canaanite cities through subversion. It was much easier to take over a city by being let into it than it was to assault the walls with primitive weapons. It is here that Rahab came in. She harbored the Israelite spies and helped them to escape from her house in the wall. She took a double gamble. She took the risk that the king would discover her subversion and execute her, and she took the risk that the Israelite invaders would kill her along with the rest of the Canaanites. In risking her future in hope that the people of God would succeed and spare her, Rahab the harlot distinguished herself as a woman of faith.

I want to underline the element of risk in genuine faith. So often faith is confused with belief—and a very static and dogmatic kind at that, a safe assent to inherited doctrines. But true faith is a risky adventure. Jewish theologian Martin Buber puts it this way: "Religion as risk is the blood of the arteries giving life to the body; religion which believes in religion is the vein's blood which ceases to circulate." The irony is that many of us pride ourselves that our religious channels became clogged long ago. We see it as constancy and faithfulness rather than the narrow-mindedness and inertia that it is. The danger is that we will cling so tenaciously to our religion that we cannot hear the fresh things that God is saying and calling us into. "if there is nothing that can so hide the face of our fellow man as morality can," Buber continues, "there is nothing that can so hide the face of God as religion. Revelation can tolerate no perfect tense, but man in the arts of his craze for security props it up to perfectedness." God's revelation is never complete. God is always revealing more of himself, more of his will, more things for us to engage in with him. If we are not only to praise but also to share in the faith of Rahab, then we too must be willing to take risks for God in hope.

VULNERABILITY

Rahab the harlot is an exemplar not only of faith founded in hope but also a faith emerging out of vulnerability. In a sense, hope is an ingredient of faith while vulnerability is almost a prerequisite for it.

The simple truth is that only those who are vulnerable, threatened, hurting, destitute—or at least upset, frustrated, and challenged—have much need for God. "Only the sick need a physician," said Jesus in justifying the narrow scope of his ministry. Only those who hunger and thirst for a social order more righteous than the one screwing them have a need to be filled; the others are full already, full of goods and full of themselves. In his cock-eyed logic, Jesus says, "Happy are the poor and the poor in spirit, for the kingdom of God belongs to them." These are the people of faith, the vulnerable ones. Not those who contribute great sums but the widow with her mite, not the proud Pharisee but the humble toll collector, not those who say "Lord, Lord" but those who do the will of the Father—these are the ones who cling to God and yearn and strive for his reign. They are partial to God out of their need, and he is partial to them in their need. Says Swiss theological Karl Barth," God always takes his stand unconditionally and passionately on this side and this side alone: against the lofty and on behalf of the lowly; against those who already enjoy right and privilege and on behalf of those who are denied it and deprived of it."

But what of the rich? Truly, they have their reward already and are not likely to turn to God to fill their lives. Jesus says that it is harder for a rich person to enter the kingdom of God than for a camel to wriggle through the eye of a needle. The story is told of a rich young ruler who was unwilling to give up his possessions, of which he had many, to follow Jesus, and among those who do not bear the fruit of the word are the seeds which spring up and are choked by cares and riches. The last are first and the first last in the kingdom of God: the poor are filled with good things; the rich are sent empty away.

Scripture is clear about the danger of wealth. Faith comes naturally to the vulnerable and only with great difficulty to the pious and pure and strong and rich. The best exemplars of natural vulnerability are women and children, especially children. Jesus says, "Let the little children come to me and forbid them not, for of such is the kingdom of God." What is the attribute of children and those who are like children that makes them naturally gravitate towards God's kingdom? I think it is vulnerability which breeds simple trust and faith.

Jesus also reaches out to women, especially to shady and broken women. I think it is significant that he is never put off by their shadiness but always zeroes in on their brokenness as a wounded healer. In a time when there was a taboo on talking with strange women in public, Jesus does not hesitate to converse about salvation with the woman at the well, who has three strikes against her: she is a Samaritan, a woman and a slut.

Jesus refuses to stone a woman taken in adultery but tells her to go and sin no more. In contrast to the inhospitable Pharisee, Jesus commends the woman of the streets who bursts unto the dinner party and anoints Jesus' head and feet, declaring she is forgiven much because she loved much—just as Jesus commended the penitent toll collector over the self-righteous Pharisee.

Because the invulnerable Pharisees give only lip service or pursue trivial morality, the toll collectors and harlots who actually show repentance and gratitude and love will enter the kingdom of God before them. These are the vulnerable ones who exhibit faith and the fruits of faith. Even Jesus' ancestry is full of shady women. Four of the five women listed in the genealogy Matthew gives Jesus are shady or disreputable or strange. Closest to Jesus is Mary, his mother, who is pregnant out of wedlock (though engaged to Joseph). Next is Bathsheba, identified as the wife of Uriah. Next comes Ruth, an alien from Moab. And finally Rahab, who is none other than our old friend Rahab the harlot, who is identified by her occupation though not to condemn her. Because of our modern preoccupation with sexual morality, we are tempted to read back into the Bible attitudes which are not there. The Bible is simply not very concerned with sexuality as such. The Bible condemns attempted homosexual rape in Sodom because it is a violation of the dignity and hospitality due to guests; it condemns male masturbation as a wasting of semen needed for procreation; it condemns adultery as stealing another man's wife; it condemns cult prostitution because of its use in the fertility rites of idolatrous pagan religion. Although ordinary harlotry frequently serves as a negative analogy for Israel's faithlessness to God, it is rarely if ever explicitly condemned in the Old Testament, and it is noteworthy that Rahab is never censured for her profession. The point in mentioning Rahab's harlotry is not to underscore her alleged immorality but to indicate her degraded social position. Rahab is scum, the lowest of the low—just as St. Paul describes the early church: the refuse and off-scourings of the world. God uses scum to do his work. These are the vulnerable ones, the desperate ones, the ones with nothing to lose in the present world order and are ready to bring in a new order, the ones who are willing to take the risk to do God's will. Few people choose to become prostitutes. In Thailand, when there is famine in the countryside, there is an upsurge of prostitutes in Bangkok. People are driven to prostitution when there is nothing left for them to sell except their own bodies. It is far too easy to condemn the prostitute as an individual sinner rather than denouncing the social system which produces prostitution. But the Bible actually praises one prostitute, Rahab the harlot, who, because of her vulnerability, risked her life to do God's will as a woman of faith.

But what about ourselves? How should we be inspired by the example of Rahab the harlot? Should we become vulnerable, give up the possessions that protect us and make us invulnerable (as Jesus advised the rich young ruler), even become prostitutes ourselves? Of course, this last would be carrying the example too far: Rahab did not choose to be a harlot and neither should we. But we do have the example of Jesus, who did not snatch at equality with God but humbled and emptied himself becoming a servant faithful even to death, seeing greatness in being servant of all. I do not know what forms of vulnerability would be most appropriate for you and for me, but I do pass on the biblical message that it is out of the vulnerability of scum like, Rahab, Jesus, and the early church that true faith is likely to arise.

ACTION

Rahab the harlot is an exemplar not only of faith founded in hope and emerging out of vulnerability but also of faith expressed in action. We are often tempted to settle for an inactive faith, lured perhaps by a reduction of the message of St. Paul to "believe and be saved." I call this "cosmic life insurance:" the premium is agreeing to mouth certain doctrinal formulas; the payoff is eternal life in heaven after death. This view distorts both the meaning of belief and of salvation. Believing for St. Paul is primarily trust in God rather than assent to doctrines. Salvation in the Old Testament is a here-and-now experience of deliverance or rescue as in the exodus or a tight battle. As Christians we may want to add an appendix on salvation, but we should never forget its original meaning. When people in the Old Testament were saved by God, they were already striving to their utmost when God added the margin of victory. You've got to be already fleeing the Egyptians—acting in faith—before God will open up a way of safety for you ("safe" comes from "salvus"). Too easily we dote on otherworldly salvation and let God do it when God is calling us, as he called Rahab the harlot, to change the world in faithfulness to him. True faith is active. The Epistle of James puts to rest the notion that you can have a living faith but not do anything about it, a notion based on a misreading of St. Paul. Faith without works is dead and barren, James bluntly states. The faith of Abraham was active along with his works and was completed by them. "And in the same way," James tell us, "Rahab the harlot was justified by works when she received the messengers and sent them out another way." Rahab had a job to do and she did it. Her faith was exercised in acts of rebellion, lying, and bargaining.

Rahab was a rebel. Rahab represents all those Canaanites who threw in their lot with invading Israelites and their more just and egalitarian system against the tyranny of Canaanite overlords. The rebellion was centered in the vulnerable lowest classes, where we have located Rahab; her prostitution was symptomatic of a wider destitution pervasive in oppressive Canaanite society. In the rising of the wretched of the earth to throw off their "lawful" masters, Rahab played a crucial role in harboring the Israelite spies and helping them to escape. Hers was an act of subversion. Now "subversion" has an ugly connotation for most Americans. Like Canaanite feudalism, American domination of the world tends to be threatened by subversion and revolution so we try to suppress them in the name of law and order, forgetting our own revolutionary origins. The Bible takes a different point of view. It praises subversion when the result is greater justice. Of course, the Israelite storytellers praise Rahab because she helped their side win. But it was more than a narrow Israelite victory. By her disloyal, disorderly, unlawful act of subversion, Rahab helped all lower class Canaanites to win a fairer shake in life by going over to a regime which eliminated extortionate taxation and forced labor and let them retain more of their produce and energy. And it was also a victory for the God of the Israelites and of all peoples whose will is to make human life more humane. Rahab through her rebellion and subversion exercised her faith in such a God.

Besides her act of rebellious subversion, and indeed as one strategy within it, a second faithful act of Rahab was lying. Does this surprise you? Imagine the glee with which the storyteller recounts the way in which Rahab duped the king and had him send a posse out in hot pursuit of the spies hidden on her rooftop! Clever girl, Rahab! The Bible does not condemn her but praises her for lying. Some preachers will tell you that the Bible is full of absolute rules, but here we see a biblical heroine breaking the rules to take an action appropriate relative to the situation. I don't know if Rahab's act was technically a case of bearing false witness against a neighbor, but it surely was an instance of lying, which, as a general rule, condemned by the world's moralities. Rahab lied. But what choice did she have? If she told the truth about the whereabouts of the spies, they would have been captured and executed and the revolution retarded. But if she lied, she would spare the lives of the spies and further the cause of the revolution of the Israelites and their God. Rahab lied in a good cause. She chose the lesser evil. And by lying she expressed her faith and hope in God's victory.

Besides subversion and lying, a third faithful act of Rahab was bargaining—bargaining in good faith we might say. Much of Joshua 2 is devoted to the bargain Rahab struck with the spies. Understandably, Rahab wanted to save her skin; she looked out for her own self-interest, and no one condemned her for that. Rahab worked out a deal with the spies that she and all her household—and by extension all the other lower class Canaanites who engaged in the rebellion—would be spared when the Israelites attacked. The Israelites showed good faith by sparing those who, though foreigners, had cast their lot with them and were at their mercy. And Rahab showed her faith in them and their God by trusting them to keep their promises. "By faith" says the book of Hebrews, "Rahab the harlot did not perish."

But what of ourselves? How can the example of Rahab the harlot inspire us to engage in faithful action? Not by sheer imitation. We are not called to imitate Rahab or the saints or even Jesus but to be as faithful to God in our situation as they were in theirs. If the situation arises where you can make a decisive blow for the triumph of righteousness by subversion, lying, and bargaining, by all means do so. It is more likely, however, that you and I will be called to fight for justice in more ordinary ways. We can begin by trying to minimize our part in the injustices we are party to. We can denounce instead of sanction the evils in the world. And we can sit down and work up strategies for increasing justice, seeking to be faithful to the God who wills all people to be saved from economic destitution, military devastation and cultural decadence.

CONCLUSION

Rahab the harlot was a woman of faith. Her faith was founded in hope, emergent out of vulnerability, and expressed in action. Her hope in the promises of God for a better future led her to take risks to help that future come into being. Her vulnerability led her to reach out to God in desperation and in yearning for his new and righteous kingdom manifest in the egalitarian Israelite political and social system. Her action took shape in subversion, lying, and bargaining in order to bring in that more just regime which had God's backing. If we are inspired by Rahab the harlot and by the whole cloud of other witnesses culminating in Christ himself, then we too must take on a faith colored by hope, vulnerability, and action. We must replace belief in religion with faith as a risky adventure. We must become one with the vulnerable, in spirit or in truth, and learn from them. And we must engage in those actions which will increase justice in the world. In doing so, we too will become people of faith.

Jesus as a Non-Violent Resister

Palestine was occupied by an empire, the Roman Empire, a world domination system. The Romans ran this world, the world. Caesar was in charge. The provincial governor was in charge. The soldiers were in charge. The Gentiles lorded it over others. There was peace in the world, the pax romana, peace at the point of a sword.

The Palestinians longed for another kind of peace. They remembered a time when lower-class Canaanites had leagued with incoming Hebrews to overthrow their overlords. They put their trust in a God who toppled kings from thrones and raised up the underclass, emptying the cupboards of the rich to nourish the poor. They looked forward to the birth of a messiah, a christened king, a scion of the ever-enduring God, a wonderful counselor, who would be a prince of peace.

In a livestock-housing cave outside of Bethlehem, the house of bread, the city of David, we are told that a boy child of great promise was born to the delight of common shepherds. He was named Yeshua in hopes that he would deliver his people from oppression. He was raised in Nazareth, a village in Galilee so marginal that it was said no good could come from it.

An ascetic prophet named John came in from the desert and began baptizing people whose change of heart involved their coming clean as they moved away from being instruments of subjugation. Toll collectors, whom the Romans employed to collect import-export duties, were told not to charge more than the official rates. Roman soldiers were told to stop shakedowns and frame-ups and to be satisfied with their pay.

Saducees, who benefited from their collaboration with the Romans, and Pharisees, whose scrupulous and haughty observance of the minutiae of dietary law set them apart from the common people, were told that their elevated status was worth nothing before the bar of God's justice unless they exhibited fruits of a change of heart. John saw his mission as leveling the mountains and valleys in society so that those with surplus clothes or food would share them with those who lacked them in response to God's rule.

Jesus was baptized by John and became his disciple. When John was imprisoned by King Herod for criticizing that Roman puppet, Jesus began his own ministry by echoing John's message that the rule of God was breaking into the world to replace the Roman regime but with a more positive twist. While John stressed judgment, Jesus called on people to change their minds and believe the good news he brought. Rejecting the bread, circuses, and political domination that characterized the Romans, Jesus told his hometown synagogue that God's spirit had anointed him to bring to the poor the good news that their poverty would be reduced, to arrange for the emptying of the debtors prisons, to open the eyes of those who had been blind to their oppression and set them free from foreign occupation, and to redistribute resources because the year of God's jubilee had arrived.

Ejected from Nazareth for his radical preaching and his upholding the inclusive love of God for Gentiles as well as Jews and abandoning his inherited occupation as construction worker, Jesus went about the countryside doing good: healing and feeding and forgiving and eating and preaching.

Jesus cast a wide net in his healings. He would heal anyone any time. He healed those considered unclean, such as lepers.

He risked contamination by healing a woman with a hemorrhage. Though reluctant at first, he healed a foreigner, a Syro-Phoenician woman. He sent healing vibes to a centurion's gay lover. From a man who inhabited a graveyard, he cast out a legion of demons, perhaps raising hopes that legions of Roman soldiers would be similarly expelled. He seemed surprised by his healing power but was elated that God was newly active in healing people through him. He said: "If by the power of God I cast out demons, then has God's kingdom appeared among you." He helped a paralytic who was waiting by a pool and told another to take up his bed and walk. Jesus told people they did not have to be sick or victims.

Jesus advised people not to worry about food and clothes. They should trust God, who feeds the birds of the air generously and clothes the lilies of the field beautifully. They should seek to implement God's rule and justice first and foremost and pray to God to advance his kingdom and provide bread and debt relief. God will judge them well if they join him in feeding the hungry, clothing the naked, seeing prisoners and releasing them, visiting the sick and healing them.

On special occasions, Jesus distributed bread to the crowds who had come out to hear him, but since popularity as prophet, priest, or king would lead him away from his mission, Jesus withdrew from the crowd and this devilish temptation.

Jesus always practiced open table fellowship. He ruined his reputation by eating with toll collectors and whores. When a woman of the streets crashed a dinner party at a Pharisee's house and anointed Jesus' head with oil and his feet with tears, Jesus was not appalled like the Pharisee but grateful: the woman was forgiven much because she loved much.

Jesus said that the toll collectors and whores would enter God's kingdom before the scribes and Pharisees. He saw children naturally accepting God's care and held them up as a model for their elders. Jesus congratulated the spirited poor who devote themselves to God's rule, those who grieve now who will be consoled, the merciful who will receive mercy, the single-minded who will be close to God's heart, the non-violent who will be caretakers of the earth, the peacemakers who will be seen as God's agents, those who hunger and thirst for justice and risk imperial persecution for it, for they will feast in God's kingdom. When the kingdom comes, the world order will be overturned: the last will be first and the first last.

Jesus invited people to love the divine in her incarnation in those near you and to love your enemies. Jesus called his hearers to be like God, all-inclusive, sending sun and rain on all, loving enemies, overcoming evil with good. Belonging to God's kingdom, they are to neutralize the empire's persecution and turn it into blessing.

Jesus set aside the ancient Law of Talion, which says "An eye for an eye and a tooth for a tooth." This was a good law designed to prevent those seeking vengeance from going overboard, but it was not good enough for Jesus. He told his hearers not to retaliate against an evildoer. This does not mean they should not resist evil. Jesus constantly exposed and resisted evil, sometimes head-on, sometimes with irony, yet he did not retaliate against those who did him wrong, but asked God to forgive them.

Evil is not allowed to go unnoticed and unchecked, but is confronted through non-violent resistance. Jesus advocated engaging in guerrilla theatre to set the authorities off balance.

He suggested turning the other cheek and giving away your underwear and walking the second mile as ways in which you can stop the cycle of violence while challenging those who humiliate, oppress, and coerce you.

Jesus said, "If someone strikes you on the right cheek, turn the other cheek also." You probably think this means taking abuse submissively, but actually it is quite provocative. You need to take into account the prejudice against the left hand in the ancient world. The word for "left" in French is gauche, which means awkward and ill-mannered, and in Latin it is sinister, which sounds downright evil. Left-handed people were outcasts then (much as gay people are in some quarters today). The left hand was regarded as unclean and could not be used in interaction with another person. The backhanded slap by the right hand against the right cheek was used to humiliate a subordinate. If your superior slaps you wrongfully on the right cheek, you could slink away humiliated, perhaps cursing him under your breath, or you could hold out your right cheek for further abuse--if you think suffering is good in itself. But what if you turned your left cheek? There is no way in which he can backhand your left cheek with his right hand. He either has to hit you, as an equal, with his right fist (or palm) or walk away. You have turned the tables on him; you have taken the initiative. You are standing before him as an equal and challenging the whole domination system that makes you subordinate to him. You could almost be taunting him, as if to say: "Your first attempt to insult and humiliate me did not work. Why don't you try again?" Perhaps it will be he, your challenged superior, who will walk away in disgust.

Jesus said, "If someone sues you for your coat, give him your underwear as well." Jewish law required returning by night a coat taken in pledge for a debt since it doubled as a blanket.

But a coat taken in a lawsuit in a Roman court as payment for debt might not be returned overnight. To expose this wrong, Jesus suggests forfeiting your underwear as well. Of course, this means that you would be standing in court stark naked! Jesus can't be serious. Nakedness in front of others was regarded as detestable in the Hebrew world, but the onus fell at least as much on the viewer as the viewed. The poor debtor who takes off his underwear is saying in effect: "If you are going to strip me of my clothes, why not take all of them? If I am going to freeze overnight without my coat, why not make me freeze completely with nothing on? I am standing here naked, but it is you who should be ashamed. In exposing myself, I am really exposing the nakedness of your greed, dear creditor, and the injustice of the system which has forced me into debt." Temple officials would take up to two thirds of a Galilean peasant's harvest for tithes and taxes.

Jesus said, "If a soldier makes you carry his pack for one mile, carry it for two." Impressment by governments was common in the ancient world. It was bad enough it you had to take your turn maintaining the roads you use or were impressed into the military or household service of your own king (as happened under Solomon), but it was extra onerous if you lived under the military occupation of a foreign power and were forced to billet soldiers and carry their luggage. Roman soldiers were armed and in charge and could easily abuse power to make citizens do what they wanted. But in a civilizing and public-relations effort, the Roman authorities forbade a soldier from making anyone carry his pack for more than a mile and meted out punishment if a soldier exceeded these bounds. But what if you voluntarily keep carrying the pack for a second mile? You are making the soldier violate his own regulations and may get him in trouble. You have taken the initiative and gone beyond the rules. Is one mile really reasonable while two miles is not?

By your action, you are challenging the reasonableness
and justice of this empire dominating other peoples.

Jesus said, "It was said of old, 'You shall love your neighbor and
hate your enemy,' but I say, 'Love your enemies.' It does not
take much to love those who love you or to greet people you
know. You can expect that much even from Gentiles and from
unscrupulous toll collectors, who contract to collect export and
import duties for a fixed sum but collect considerably more
than that and pocket the surplus themselves. But it takes guts
to broaden the circle of your affections to include everyone
and to reach out to them as Jesus and his Good Samaritan did.
There is no suggestion that your enemy will love you back or
your persecutor will appreciate your prayers for him. You
might well be met with hate and continuing injustice, but that
need not stop you from loving, which is your choice and not a
reaction to the stance of others. As children of God,
commissioned to carry out God's work, you can be as God is:
perfect, complete, holy, merciful, inclusive. God is perfect and
complete because God embraces the imperfect and
incomplete. God's holiness is shown in reaching out to the
wayward in mercy. God's inclusiveness is the chief expression
of her love and is ours to imitate. As God in God's all-inclusive
love gives blessed rain and sun to all, said Jesus, so you should
be completely generous, giving to those who beg or borrow.
Even in provoking and criticizing the unjust enemy, love should
be your aim as you envision "a redeemed community" in and
beyond the struggle for justice and peace.

Jesus organized an alternative community in the midst of the
world that operated on its own rules and thereby challenged
the domination system of the Roman occupiers and of the
leaders of his own Jewish society, who were often in league
with the Romans. The leaders fell basically into two camps:

the purists, such as Pharisees and scribes, and the collaborators, such as Saducees and Herodians. While the Pharisees were famous for adding to the law until it became quite burdensome, the Saducees were "traditionalists," who adhered to only the oldest laws so they could get away with more. Jesus criticized the Pharisees' preoccupation with petty laws as a distraction from justice, mercy, and faith while the Saducees were disparaged for fostering injustice as they served the authorities without qualms as "yes men". Neither set of leaders resisted the current order, but they wore ornate robes as they sought the chief seats within it.

Jesus took the opposite approach. When two of his disciples wanted to secure places in a hierarchy asking to sit at Jesus' right and left, he would not hear of it. When he was called "good teacher," he said that none is good but God, and he instructed his disciples to call no man "rabbi" or "teacher" or "father" but to look to God for leadership. Jesus sought followers rather than worshippers and said that changing the world in accordance with God's will was the gate to God's kingdom. He humbly washed feet and told his disciples to do likewise. He said the greatest among you is the one who is servant of all. Devotion to the community took precedence over everything else including family, which it replaced. When Jesus' mother and brothers came to visit him, he ignored them saying those who follow him are family.

Jesus might have been ignored if he ran a blessed community isolated from the world, but his was a traveling expedition, which wound up in Jerusalem, the locus of the Jewish temple and the citadel of Roman power. Jesus entered Jerusalem triumphantly as a messianic king while people laid palm branches before him and sang hosannas to this son of David.

Then he caused a disturbance in the temple by a non-violent disruption of the market for sacrificial animals held there. These affronts to the ruling powers would not go unpunished.

After a night in Bethany, Jesus came back to the temple to teach about God's kingdom and to face his challengers. When Jesus was asked for the basis of his authority, he turned the question back and asked whether the authority of John the Baptist was human or divine. This stumped his questioners. If they said that John's calling was merely human, then they would lose the confidence of the people who saw John, imprisoned and since beheaded, as a martyr for God's way. And if they said John's calling was divine, they would have themselves to blame for failing to support the attempt of John and Jesus to turn the world upside down. So they backed off.

One of the collaborators, perhaps one of Herod's henchmen asked a question about taxes. You have probably heard Jesus' saying: "Render to Caesar what is Caesar's, but render to God what is God's" and you probably assumed that it meant that religion and politics inhabit different spheres. But this saying means something quite different when examined in context. The collaborator thought he could get Jesus into trouble by asking him a trick question: "Is it lawful to pay taxes to Caesar?" If Jesus told people to pay taxes, he would lose his popular following, who hated the oppressive Roman occupation and did not want to pay for it. If Jesus told people not to pay taxes, he would be arrested by the Romans even sooner for tax sedition. The collaborator thought he had Jesus over a barrel, but Jesus turned the tables on him. Because the Second Commandment forbids making engraved images, the Romans minted special coins for the Jews with no faces on them. Jesus asked the collaborator to show him a coin. The collaborator reaches into his pocket and pulls out a coin.

And lo and behold, it has Caesar's face on it: the sacred emporer Tiberias is on the front and his dead mother, who was considered a divinity, was on the back! Now it is the collaborator who is in hot water exposing his lack of scruples. When Jesus says, "Give to Caesar what is Caesar's, but give to God what is God's," he is, in effect, saying: "If you are such a bad Jew that you can be caught red-faced and red-handed with a coin bearing Caesar's face, well why don't you give that dirty old coin back to Caesar and give to God what belongs to God, which is everything."

Jesus, the non-violent resister, was arrested by the authorities. When his disciple Peter began to resist violently, Jesus told him to put his sword away since violence brings destruction to those who perpetrate it as well as those who receive it. Jesus' failure to try to oust the Romans by force was deeply disappointing to the Zealots and perplexing to the Romans, who weren't taking any chances. Pilate released Barabbas, a Zealot who led an armed insurrection, as less of a threat than Jesus. At his trial, Jesus was accused of being a rival to Caesar, which he was. When asked whether he was a king, Jesus said that if his kingdom was just another form of the domination system of the sort the Romans ran, then his servants would fight; instead, he aimed to eliminate domination and violence altogether. Jesus was executed by Rome with an indictment sign reading "Jesus of Nazareth, King of the Jews." On the cross, he forgave his executioners.

Repentance

John the Baptizer and Jesus of Nazareth said the same thing, "Repent, for the rule of God is at hand," but they meant very different things. The irony is that the church aims and claims to follow Jesus but, in fact, often follows John instead. Take fasting. John the Baptist and his disciples fasted, but Jesus' disciples defended their _not_ fasting because why would they fast when the bridegroom is still with them. And why would we fast if the risen bridegroom is with us? And yet the church sets aside a penitential season of Lent with fasting and giving things up and mortification of the flesh. Just before Lent there is great fun in Mardi Gras, which means the Fat Tuesday which precedes Ash Wednesday, or in Carnival, Carne-vale, farewell to flesh. But why should we identify this exuberance with sin and the moroseness of Lent as more spiritual? If the Word became flesh, what can be wrong with flesh?

John the Baptizer was an austere desert prophet who rang down God's judgment. He regarded the good man as like a tree planted by a river that brings forth good fruit in its season. He demanded that those who came to him for baptism for forgiveness of sins exhibit fruits worthy of repentance. A man who has two coats must give one to someone who is coatless and likewise with food. A toll collector must avoid overcharging. Roman soldiers must stop bullying, blackmail and extortion. The axe is ready to fell the tree without fruit. The grim reaper is coming, said John, who will blow away the wicked like chaff and consume them with unquenchable fire. Jesus did not turn out at all like this.

If Jesus and John were so different from each other in who they were and what they meant, how come they both said the same thing? I believe this happened because Jesus was a disciple of John baptized by John to wash away his sins. In their curious logic, biblical scholars are convinced that Jesus was actually baptized by John because it is such an embarrassment to the Gospel writers, who engaged in great feats of interpretation to explain why it was not what it seemed: a baptism for forgiveness of sins.

If you are steeped in trinitarian thinking, then you learn from John's Gospel that God the Son as the Word of God was active in creation and spoke through the prophets and became incarnate in Jesus. From Luke you can add a miraculous virgin birth. What you end up with is the absurd conception of God in diapers with Jesus as some kind of non-human boy wonder with divine powers zapping children who irked him (in tales rightly excluded from the canon of scripture).

I think that Jesus was a real boy and a real young man, who took up his father's occupation of construction worker and did not begin his ministry until he was about age 30. Was Jesus busy being God all that time? Was he sinless for his first 30 years? I doubt it. I do not require a sinless Jesus. You need one only if you subscribe to a substitutionary atonement theory in which God tortures his totally innocent Son as a replacement for giving sinners like us the punishment we deserve. This is a monstrous theory in my view; my God is not like that. And I think the God that Jesus believed in and exemplifies in not like that either.

Jesus was a disciple of John baptized by John to wash away his sins. That's why people came to John for baptism. But what is sin or sins? The classic theological tradition from Augustine on holds that sin is separation from God and that sins are symptoms rooted in this separation. When we get out of touch with God, we go astray; we "miss the mark" to use the archery analogy beneath the New Testament word for sin. Or as Barak Obama put it, sin means "being out of alignment with my values." We do what we should not do and fail to do what we should; we commit sins of commission and sins of omission. Cure sin, and sins go away. Jesus was, no doubt, a good and pious Jew. He went to synagogue and studied the scriptures perhaps even had a precocious knowledge of it. But something was missing, and Jesus went to John for baptism.

There is no evidence that Jesus committed any particular sins when young. But he would not have gone to John for baptism unless he thought he needed to be closer to God and more involved with God's work. The baptism of Jesus, at the very least, confirms a conversion, a turning toward God in a fuller way. The Gospel writers take it up a notch, and rightly so, by seeing Jesus' baptism also as an anointing by God's Spirit and thus a commissioning to serve God in a new way. After rejecting temptations to engage in economic, religious, or political spectacles, Jesus told his hometown synagogue that in this ripe time God's Spirit had anointed him to relieve poverty, blindness, captivity, and oppression. Jesus was called to give the world a make-over, and he, in turn, called others to join him in this process of saving the world.

The disciples did not have to leave theirs sins but leave their nets. Jesus does not analyze their shortcomings but calls them to get on board, to get with the program. It is not wrong to fish for fish; it feeds you and others. It is not wrong to have a new wife; it is wonderful. It is not wrong to plow a field;

it is needed. It is not wrong to bury a father; it is a familial duty. But Jesus calls people away from these good things to follow him: to be fishers of men, to join a new family, to labor in God's vineyard, to bury the old self and emerge renewed. While John was austere as he called cads to escape God's wrath by leaving misdeeds in favor of just wages and sharing, Jesus was convivial inviting people to change their whole way of thinking and see God's rule breaking into the world as good news to be celebrated and extended. The repentance Jesus favors is literally changing your mind ["meta-noia" in New Testament Greek]. While John is a puritan who drinks no wine, Jesus is a man who eats and drinks as friend with cheats and sluts. No prophet is greater than John, but anyone who takes part in God's royal wedding banquet has surpassed John.

Jesus proclaims and embodies a God who is full of grace. In the teaching of Jesus, God makes his blessings of sun and rain to fall on the just and the unjust, and people are invited to be all-inclusive as God is all-inclusive. In Jesus' parable, the prodigal son is full of self-loathing and his older brother would stoke that fire, but the father will hear nothing of it; he runs out to welcome back his lost son and throws a party. The account of Jesus at the home of Simon the Pharisee is most telling. The Pharisee is aghast at the prostitute who crashes his dinner party to anoint Jesus' head with oil and to wash his feet with her tears; Jesus is not put off by her sins but taken by her love; she is forgiven much because she loved much. Love cancels and replaces a multitude of sins. Love keeps no score of wrongs; it does not gloat over the sins of others but delights in what is being done right. Love accentuates the positive.

Leadership styles can vary from the punitive father at one end to the nurturing mother at the other. In both his character and his depiction of God, John the Baptizer portrayed the punitive father while Jesus exemplified the nurturing mother. When Jerusalem proved unresponsive to him, Jesus cried: "Jerusalem! Jerusalem! Killing all the prophets. How would I have loved to gather you as a hen gathers her chicks under her wings, but you would not." Jesus leads by encouragement and example rather than ordering. He told his disciples, "The Gentiles lord it over one another, but it shall not be so among you. Whoever is servant is greatest of all." Jesus advocated humility and service but also exemplified it. After washing his disciples' feet Jesus said, "If I your Lord and Master washed your feet, you also ought to wash one another's feet."

In attempting to serve and help, ministers and counselors and other people can be punitive or clinical or nurturing. In her book "Conjoint Family Therapy," Virginia Satir lays out three frameworks for therapy: sin, sickness, and growth.

In the sin frame, a person is blamed and condemned for their misdeeds and told to change. But as Joseph Campbell, author of "The Power of Myth," points out, those preoccupied with sins remain sinners. Sinning easily becomes a rut. Those who feel guilty feel so bad about themselves that they will not change. The sickness frame seems like a step ahead. Now instead of cussing out a person who drinks too much as a "damned drunk," he can be regarded as a victim of the disease of alcoholism. But pity does not enable change either. A pathetic person still feels powerless. The growth frame is best. Here the counselor regards a person with problems as capable and encourages her to take action. Jesus uses the growth frame. In the case of a man born blind, he avoids blaming either the man or his parents. And to the man who had lain for years by the pool of Bethsaida, he says, "Take up your bed and walk!"

I spent my early ministry working for civil rights first with a black Baptist church in inner-city Cleveland and later with Project Understanding, which helped six white churches in California know and deal with their white racism. In the training for Project Understanding, we examined four different emotions that might hamper or contribute to solving the race problem: fear, guilt, anger, and activism. Fear is crippling and breeds avoidance and defensiveness. During the Hough riots in Cleveland, the suburban volunteers at our preschool stayed away out of fear and were understandably not reassured when I said, "We only riot at night." Guilt moves a little ahead but bogs people down. People become preoccupied with what is wrong and overwhelmed by it even if they are willing to acknowledge their own complicity with it deliberately or inadvertently. Anger is a more rousing emotion and can be somewhat productive when it is directed at the world that has deformed us through racism, but it easily becomes engulfing as one directs blame at others. I have a friend who is angry all the time, and this alienates colleagues and hampers the work of seeking justice. A spirit of activism is best because it motivates actually taking steps to change.

John the Baptizer relied on each of these emotions. He evoked lots of fear as he proclaimed the imminent judgment of a punitive God. He laid plenty of guilt on people as he confronted them as sinners in need of a baptism of forgiveness. He was an angry prophet who blamed the Pharisees and called then a brood of snakes. He also demanded commitment to action, such as sharing food and clothes and not taking advantage of other people.

Jesus is much more positive. He emphasizes action. In his account of a last judgment, Jesus does not evoke fear of punishment or praise penitent groveling or get angry or even demand action. He merely commends those who naturally and unwittingly do what needs to be done to care for the least, those most in need, by feeding the hungry, clothing the naked, quenching thirst, visiting those who are sick and in prison, and he tags them as belonging to God's kingdom. This Kingdom of God is the new thing breaking into the world. It changes everything. Jesus says: "The time is fulfilled. The Kingdom of God is at hand. Repent, change your mind, and believe this good news." This is the Jubilee, the year of God's favor, when the Spirit moves Jesus and his followers to relieve poverty, blindness, captivity, and oppression, not through angry denunciation but through loving service, indiscriminate healing, and non-violent resistance.

In the Greek this kingdom of God is "basileia theou," the empire of God, standing over against the empire of Caesar. But it is a very anti-imperialist empire. It does not feature a God who is a cosmic tyrant demanding obedience but rather a God who invites and inspires as exemplified in the way of Jesus, a poor and humble peasant, soon to be ground up in the gears of imperial justice. Jesus exalts love as supreme inviting followers to love God and neighbor as yourself. If we concentrate on love, we don't have to worry about sins. Saint Paul, who said that love is greater than even faith and hope, said: "Owe no one anything but love, for love is the fulfillment of the law." Jesus disdained those who were convinced of their own sanctity and welcomed those who were tagged as sinners. He told the Pharisees that whores and toll collectors were entering God's kingdom before them. He healed lepers, who were considered unclean, and he healed the gay lover of a faith-filled Roman centurion. He turned a despised Samaritan into the hero of a parable because he reached out lovingly to a man beat up by thieves while a priest and a Levite passed him by. There are three reasons Jesus should not talk to the woman at the well: she is a Samaritan; she is a woman; and she has had seven husbands. But Jesus does not focus on her shortcomings but encourages her to proclaim him as bread of life and living water. For God loved the world so much that he sent Jesus not to condemn the world for its sins but to save the world for a life of joy and love.

There is a very strange and poignant passage in the Gospel of Luke that spells out the difference between John the Baptizer and Jesus and rues that people did not respond well to either one:

This generation is like children sitting in the marketplace and shouting at each other, "We piped for you, and you would not dance. We wept and wailed, and you would not mourn." For John the Baptizer came neither eating bread nor drinking wine, and you say, "He is possessed." The son of man came eating and drinking, and you say, "Look at him! A glutton and a drinker, a friend of toll collectors and sinners." Yet wisdom is justified by all her children. [Luke 7:31-35]

Most people do not listen to John's dirge or join in Jesus' dance. But if we are to choose, I would go with Jesus. Jesus said that "no prophet is greater than John," but the kingdom of God as Jesus proclaims it is so wonderful that Jesus also said, "whoever is least in the kingdom of God is greater than John." John the Baptizer focused on sins. Jesus did not. So I say, "Forget sin." As Paul says, "There is no condemnation for those who are in Christ Jesus." John calls for self-sorry penitence, but Jesus calls for life-changing repentance.

Hearts and Ashes (Song of Songs 5:19-16; 7:1-13; John 15:1-17)

Occasionally, Valentine's Day and Ash Wednesday crop up in the same week, each with its distinctive take on love. Love is central in Christianity. In John's Gospel, Jesus commanded his disciples to love one another. In the synoptic tradition, the great invitations are to love God with all your heart, soul and mind and to love your neighbor as yourself. St. Paul identifies the Christian virtues as faith, hope, and love, and he says the greatest of these is love. The author of I John states that God is love. Endorsement for love in popular culture is also legion.

Love seems to be much sought but little achieved. Says Erich Fromm: "There is hardly any activity, any enterprise which is started with such tremendous hopes and expectations, and yet which fails so regularly, as love." Love seems to be much praised but little understood. At one level, love is the simplest and most natural thing in the world, but it is also complicated; love is complex, indeed multiplex. In his book "The Colors of Love," Alan John Lee identifies nine types of love. Ludus (blue) is playful love, love as a game, even replete sometimes with the notion of "scoring;" since it involves so little commitment, ludus is hardly a form of love though it is one way to use sex. Mania (purple) is love as madness, characterized by falling in love and out of it, a roller coaster love of the heart which is often heartsick with heartache. Pragma (green) is a non-romantic, practical love based on economic and social considerations; it is the norm in much of the world where marriages are arranged and personalized love may be expected to develop in time.

Deeper than these three types of love are three types we will explore in detail: eros, storge, and agape. Briefly, eros is passionate love of an idealized object; storge is slow-burning love of a companion; agape is persistent self-giving love for all.

Much of Christian preaching has been anti-erotic, but I would like to give the erotic its due and make a balanced presentation. I will be drawing on three parallel schemes. First is Alan John Lee's colors of love in which the red of eros and the yellow of storge are blended and transcended by the orange of agape. Second, Freud recognized two great forces in life, Eros and Thanatos, Love and Death, combined, I say, in Communion. Third Gail Sheehy in her book on human development entitled "Passages" speaks of a seeker self and a merger self, integrated and fulfilled in mutuality.

Before the genesis of Eros the world is lifeless both for nature and for the infant. Writes Rollo May:

> In the early Greek account of creation, Eros—Love—creates life upon earth. He seizes life-giving arrows and pierces the cold bosom of earth and immediately the brown surface is covered with luxuriant verdure. Before all is silent, bare, and motionless. Now all is life, joy, and motion.

For the very young child there is security in being an undifferentiated part of its parental milieu, and the first stirrings of eros may be experienced as a fall from primeval innocence, but it also begins the journey of becoming a person in his or her own right. The seeker self is assertive, renegade, and curious, wanting to be not only with parents but also like them, strong and independent. Eros underlies the impulse to make something of yourself, to wash things and people with your love or what Freud called libido. At bottom, Eros is "polymorphously perverse," seeking pleasure wherever it can (Freud), but in its ultimate reaches Eros can set almost unattainably high standards. "Erotic lovers are on a demanding search for their ideal of beauty," writes Alan John Lee. Eros is the stuff of dreams, as reflected in a suitor saying "he was as I dreamed he would be." An erotic encounter is often marked by an almost chemical reaction, including more rapid heartbeat, making eros literally a matter of the heart. Eros delights in a sensual feeling for the beautiful body and revels in intimacy, self-revelation, and confidence. Erotic love is for the "lucky and the strong."

The love which popular songs endlessly celebrate tends to focus on the erotic quest, sometimes with ludic overtones. The notion that love is to be concentrated exclusively on an outstanding person is frequently sounded from the biblical Song of Songs, where the bride calls the bridegroom "a paragon among ten thousand and wholly desirable," to "The Rose," where love is a flower and "you its only seed." While "The Rose" denies that love is only for the lucky and the strong and paints love in many colors, most popular songs are monochromatic in their treatment of love, and in their saturation-repetition of a narrow range, they become trite and boring. Commenting on our contemporary culture, Rollo May concludes, "Eros has lost passion and become insipid, childish, and banal." Besides becoming dispirited and debased, Eros also has serious drawbacks: it can become insatiable, dangerous, and fleeting.

Eros feeds on fantasy, and erotic fantasy objects are often so splendid as to make real people fall far short by comparison. There is no satisfying Eros; it is a "hunger, an endless aching need," says "The Rose," reflecting on Eros tinged with mania. We will never find the perfect mate, nor are we perfect ourselves.

Eros can wield overwhelming power, like "a river that drowns the tender reed," or it can be painful like a razor that cuts and abandons. Some of Eros' (or Cupid's) arrows are poisoned.

Nor does Eros age well. People who fall in love can also fall out of love. A popular song speaks of the "elusive butterfly of love." Erotic love does not last forever except in dreams and fairy tales where Prince Charming and his wife live happily ever after. Says John Donne in one of his poems: "the moment after noon is night."

Despite its drawbacks in terms of instability, insatiability, and danger and its limitations when pursued monochromatically, Eros is an essential ingredient in a full spectrum of loves. Says Rollo May:

> Sexual love requires self-assertion. If we cannot be individuals in our own right, we have nothing to give, nothing to relate with. Unable to assert ourselves, we cannot participate genuinely in a relationship.

Storge seeks an eternal return, a return to the cultural or personal world before differentiation set in. The merger self hankers after fusion, restoring "beatific closeness with mother, replete with perfect harmony, absolute safety, and endless time (Sheehy)." The merger self wants complete security from womb to tomb, wants to go back to the womb or on to the watery grave of death, to experience what Freud calls the "oceanic feeling." This is Thanatos, the death force. This is Hamlet's wish that "this too, too sullied flesh might melt," that he might find relief from the burdens of life—from the "slings and arrows of outrageous fortune"—in the sleep of death. Yet the death wish need not be literally suicidal; it may wish only a temporary surcease, a respite, a taste and not a full draught of oblivion, the death not of a person but of a separated self. This sort of death wish is at the heart of Eastern religions and Western mysticism as well.

Hinduism teaches that the apparent multiplicity of things in the world is an illusion, that all are one including self and divinity ("atman is brahman"), that fulfillment lies in the absorption of self into the All-Soul. Buddhism teaches that the self is an illusion, that there is no soul ("an-atta"), and it counsels non-striving and detachment from personal relationships while feeling compassion for all living beings as the path to salvation, conceived as relief from suffering. In a culture which stresses striving, making somethings of yourself, becoming a self-made man or woman, and measuring worth by accomplishments and productivity by activity, there is some appeal in the Eastern alternatives at least as an antidote; Daniel Berrigan reversed a familiar American maxim along Buddhist lines when he said, "Buddha says, 'Don't just do something; stand there.'" Americans, however, are more likely to use alcohol and other drugs to escape the pain of a fully conscious life rather than mysticism though a few join cults to evade responsibility for decisions. Lovemaking can also express the death wish of the merger self, seeking to be embraced, to be engulfed, to lose the self in the arms of the lover.

Storge encompasses more than Thanatos but remains enshrouded by it in its search for peace and tranquility rather than adventure and challenge. Storge is "love without fever, tumult, or folly, a peaceful and enchanting affection," wrote Proudhon. It is a slow-burning love, uncharred with flames of passion, in which the sexual element in loving tends to be downplayed. Storgic love is unaware of intense feeling, unsentimental and unromantic, coming naturally with the passage of time and sharing of activities, friendship, and companionship; it is a kind of brotherly love, not far from philia, which some of you may have run into in the usual triad of eros, philia, and agape. Storge develops in the context of marriage, home, and child-raising. In cultures where marriages are arranged by parents, often for primarily pragmatic reasons, rather than initiated by lovers on the basis of erotic attraction, love of a storgic sort is expected to be the outcome of marriage; in "Fiddler on the Roof" Golda cites twenty-five years of washing his clothes as proof of her love for Tievyev when confronted with the silly question, "Do I love you?" In our culture eros tends to come first and storge later; some spouses actually become better friends once they cease to be erotic lovers or even after divorce. In a youth-worshiping culture, storge is rarely celebrated or even recognized as a form of love. An exception is a song which states that love is more comfortable the second time around. "On Golden Pond" portrays mature, old-hat, cantankerous love between two old people.

Like eros, storge has its drawbacks, but of an opposite sort. While eros can breed too much intensity, storge may generate too little. Erotic lovers are subject to overwhelming passions and a heartsick worry based on instability and verging on mania; storgic lovers are liable to develop an "old shoe" feeling and to take each other for granted. Storge can be humdrum, stifling, and boring, rather like the boring Heaven which the general in Shaw's "Man and Superman" abandons because nothing goes wrong there to liven it up. Some couples pride themselves on never being cross with each other, but psychologists rate frequent focused fair fights as healthier than repressed anger and accumulating resentments which encumber a seemingly placid relationship. A love afraid of conflict and risk is repeatedly bemoaned in "The Rose:" the unbreakable heart never dances; no chances are taken in a perpetual dream; you dissipate your capacity to give if you are constantly on guard lest someone take advantage of you. Lonely nights and long roads can discourage the timid soul, and the spectre of love as an engulfing river or bloody razor can induce the storgic lover to renounce Eros and take refuge in Thanatos.

I'm afraid the Christian Church is guilty of fostering such renunciation: with its glorification of celibate priest, monks, and nuns; with its somber observance of Ash Wednesday and Lent emphasizing penitence and humility; with its uncritical denunciation of selfishness and exaltation of self-sacrifice; with what Nietzsche calls its "slave morality" abjuring pride and exulting in self-effacing obedience. The church needs to give up its preoccupation with death and learn to love life without fear, to teach us to love our neighbors as ourselves and not instead of ourselves, to induce us to give _of_ ourselves rather than give _up_ selves we were afraid to grow.

Despite its drawbacks in terms of inertia, boredom, and selflessness and its limitations when pursued monochromatically, storge is an essential ingredient in a full spectrum of loves. While premature burial of self benefits no one, mature love requires give and take. Even sexual love, which we conceive mainly in erotic terms requires a degree of storgic self-giving, death, and merger. Says Rollo May, "The capacity for surrender, for giving one's self up must exist in lovemaking if there is to be the spontaneity for orgasm." The answer lies in neither eros or storge alone but in their combination, transmuted by agape. To love fully, we need to balance self-assertion and self-sacrifice, love and death, hearts and ashes, seeker self and merger self, eros and storge.

Alan John Lee in "The Colors of Love" recognizes three combination loves including Erotic-Storgic, which he describes as integrating the intense emotion of eros with the enduring patience and abiding affection of storge. Conquest yields to surrender when you catch a mate so you can lose yourself in the other's arms; self-abandonment for purposes of merger can be a means to self-realization, parallel to Jesus' paradoxical saying that "he who loses his life for my sake will gain it."

The true aim of love, according to Gail Sheehy, is neither seeking nor merging alone but their resolution in mutuality, or in theological terms, in communion. Communion, whether communion with god or a human lover, involves union with, neither dominating or being dominated. Although it is difficult to make much sense of it in a literal way, the Christian creedal affirmation of the "resurrection of the body" functions to confirm the goodness of our bodies and of our separate identities. In contrast to the Hindu view of salvation as absorption into the Godhead, Judaism and Christianity depict salvation in terms of reciprocal love between God and humans. Likewise, the biblical model of sexual union is "two persons becoming one flesh"—without ceasing to be two persons. This motif if beautifully expressed in a poem by Khalil Gibran, which I use in weddings:

> Let there be spaces in your togetherness,
> And let the winds of the heavens dance between you.
> Love one another, but make not a bond of love;
> Let it rather be a moving sea between your souls.
> Sing and dance together and be joyous,
> But let each of you also be alone,
> Even as the strings of a lute are alone
> Though they quiver with the same music.
> And stand together, yet not too near together;
> For the pillars of the temple stand apart,
> And the oak tree and the cypress grow not in each other's shadow.

Both eros and storge are leery of conflict, which has no place in storybook romance or companionship. Erotic love is blind to faults, and storgic love sweeps conflicts under the rug to keep peace; neither is tough enough to face conflicts and work them through, encompassing and overcoming negativity, death and evil.

It is here that agape comes in, completing and transcending eros and storge in its ability to love under pressure of adverse circumstances. Agape invites reciprocity but keeps on loving whether there is a positive response or not. Unlike storge's cousin, philia, agape loves enemies as well as friends and loves both unstintingly. "Greater love has no man," says the Gospel of John, "than to lay down his life for his friends." Agape is self-giving love, not a love which gives up the self or has no self to give but a love which actualizes self through the process of giving. Agape is a sacrificial love, not in the negative sense of sacrifice as giving something up but in the positive meaning of sacri-ficium, making holy; agape is a love which creates holiness, which makes the wounded whole.

We see agapic love supremely in Jesus, whom Theologian Dietrich Bonhoeffer calls "the man for others." Indeed, it is Jesus being-for-others that makes him a revelation of the holy God, for the transcendence of God does not lie in his almighty power but in the depth of his love, which we see enacted most clearly in Jesus. "God is love," says the First Epistle of John. Where there is love, there is God. This is what we mean by 'God,' this transcendent love at work in the world. This is what we worship, what we consider to be of supreme worth; we do not revere a supreme supernatural being but serve God by letting his love be shed abroad in our hearts through the holy spirit at work in us.

Being channels of God's agape may involve sacrifice in the negative sense. It certainly did for Jesus and his disciples and apostles. Jesus was crucified, his disciples persecuted, St. Paul beaten, jailed, expelled, all for love. A slogan of the early church was: "The blood of the martyrs is the seed of the church." Even St. Valentine was a martyr slain by the Romans in 269 A.D.

Ash Wednesday and the Lenten season commemorate the sacrifice of Jesus and the martyrs; ashes symbolize humiliation and degradation. Holy Communion is a participation in the sacrifice of Christ, and baptism symbolizes not only his death and resurrection but also that of believers. Unfortunately, Ash Wednesday has become a somber rite of penitence, communion a mystical ritual, and baptism a sentimental baby ceremony. Jesus said, "I came that my joy might be in you and your joy might be full, that you might abide in my love and bear much fruit." The holy love which Jesus taught far exceeded in positive worth the negative sufferings which came with it as sufferings became transmuted into joy.

The Christian message is not that there are hearts and ashes but that somehow the two are the same, just as St. Valentine was a martyred lover and Jesus a loving victim/victor. Christ crucified exhibit the paradox of undying love in the very process of love dying, and the ignominious cross has been transfigured into a symbol of triumph. Secular wisdom tells us that after winter comes spring. In "The Rose" we are admonished to "remember in the winter far beneath the bitter snows lies the seed that with the sun's love in the spring becomes the rose." But Christian wisdom asserts that winter is spring and darkness light as we sing of the nativity of Jesus:

> Lo, how a rose e'er blooming
> From tender stem has sprung.
> Of Jesse's lineage coming
> As men of old have sung.
> It came a flow'ret bright
> Amid the cold of winter
> When half-spent was the night.

What are we to do with all of this? I think we should examine our own styles of loving, see how much we engage in eros or storge or agape. Perhaps we could expand our repertoire of loves and the circles of our affections. Perhaps we could achieve a new balance if we have been rather monochromatic, take fresh risks if we have been constrained.

We are challenged and invited by the example, presence, and community of Christ to give of ourselves in holy love, to practice communion. My brothers and sisters, let us love in deed and in truth, for all love is of God. A Taize chant affirms: "Ubi caritas et amor, ubi caritas, deus ibi est." Where there is sacrificial love and romantic love, wherever there is love, there is God.

Making Love Paramount (Matthew 22:34-40, Romans 13:8-10)

0. Introduction

The General Assembly of the Presbyterian Church (USA) met in mid-June
of 1991. One report it received with thanks but declined to adopt
was entitled "Keeping Body and Soul Together: Sexuality,
Spirituality, and Social Justice." This report has become, as
Newsweek put it, a "Presbyterian best seller" with more than
42,000 copies sold. The report has elicited a swirl of controversy,
with many attacking it, often injudiciously, and a few praising it as a
major breakthrough. The majority report is accompanied by six
additional statements from committee members partially
disagreeing with the majority, bundled into a minority report. I
myself have read most of and appreciated much in both reports,
attended a Whitewater Valley Presbytery forum on the topic, sent
letters to our commissioners expressing my views and prayers, and
am using the sexuality report as backdrop for this morning's
sermon. The report has been attacked as unscriptural because it
elevates love and justice above conventional moral prescriptions. I,
however, find it very much in the best of our Reformed tradition to
make Jesus Christ and his teaching on the primacy of love central.
In response to the content of, and controversy about, the sexuality
report, I will be asserting three things this morning:

> 1) that the love of God for us as Creator-Redeemer-Sustainer is the
>   heart of the gospel
> 2) that the commandments to love God and neighbor
>   take precedence over all other commandments
> 3) that all of scripture is dependent on these two commandments
>   and is to be interpreted in light of them.

1. The Love of God for us

God's graciousness and love precede all commandments. We see this in
the preface to Ten Commandments: I am the Lord your God who delivered
you from slavery in Egypt. We love because he first loved us; we give
God's love back to him. God so loved the world that he gave his son,
not to condemn the world but so the world through him might be saved.
God is our creator, giving gifts to all of us, including the gift of sexuality.

As the song says, "He's got the whole world in his hands." God makes a world where some people have disabilities. God makes a world where people have different sexual orientations. God makes a world in which we go through successive life cycle stages. Some days we may say, "O God, I don't want to be old," but that is part of his design for our lives. Every one of us--disabled and able, gay and straight, old and young--is a beloved child of God, blessed with ability to experience intimacy. God is love; all love is of God; all love is good.

The Greeks distinguish three kinds of love: <u>agape</u>, <u>philia</u>, and <u>eros</u>. Agape is self-giving love; philia is friendship; eros is sexual love. God is the author of all these loves. As an ancient plainsong puts it: "Ubi caritas et amor, ubi caritas, deus ibi est." Where there is charitable love and amorous love, wherever there is love, there is God.

God has an erotic relationship to the universe he spawns. God is fertile, the fount of possibilities for creatures (Whitehead). Like Jesus, we are all of the Father's love begotten. Ours is a sex-saturated culture, yet it has too little, not too much, eros. In his critique of Playboy, Harvey Cox sees American males enamored of pretty pictures with a staple in the middle but scared of deep engagement with flesh-and-blood people. Most of our pornography is—as an earlier report to the General Assembly put it--"far from the Song of Songs," (formerly called Song of Solomon), where erotic love is celebrated in its fullness.

The first thing to be said is that God loves us and that his love is the source of all our loves. The primacy of the good news of God's love over morality is clearly proclaimed in Jesus' story of the prodigal son, where the older brother is plenty moral and the younger plenty sinful yet the loving father runs out and embraces his returning younger son.

2. Our Loving God and Neighbor

The commandments to love God and to love your neighbor originated in different parts of the Old Testament. The commandment to love God is given great prominence in Deuteronomy 6, where it follows the Ten Commandments. It is directly preceded there by an assertion of monotheism, "Hear, O Israel, the Lord our God, the Lord is one"--
a preface retained in rendering this commandment in Mark's version.

The commandment to love your neighbor as yourself comes from Lev. 18, where it is sandwiched in without emphasis between commandments to honor parents and keep the sabbath and provide for poor and blind and a commandment not to wear clothes made of two fabrics.

When Jesus replies to a scribe that these love commandments are primary, he is not met by surprise at originality but by confirmation (Mark12:32), with the scribe adding that love is more important than sacrifices. In Luke 10, it is not Jesus but the lawyer who states the love commands, which Jesus then amplifies by telling the Good Samaritan story.   In that story, it is not the priest or Levite, who keep ritual laws but leave the robbed man in the ditch, but the Samaritan, whose people break laws by intermarrying and by worshiping on Mount Gerazim, who is commended for keeping the important command by being kind to the robbed man. In Matthew 22, Jesus follows the commands by asserting that all of scripture is subordinate to them. Thus in each of the contexts for the great commands in the synoptic Gospels, we see Jesus not only endorsing the importance of the love commands, which is what we will deal with now, but also downgrading other commandments by comparison, which we will explore in greater detail later.

We are called first to love God for his own sake, out of gratitude. But because God is the ground of our own being, to love God is to also to love our own selves and to extend that love beyond ourselves to our neighbors. How can you love God whom you have not seen, says the book of James, if you do not love your brother whom you have seen? Loving involves seeking justice for another as for ourselves. God wants us to do justice, love mercy, and walk humbly with him (Micah). Justice, mercy, and faith fit together, for walking with God involves doing justice and mercy. Jesus is the Way--the way for us to walk--as well as the truth and the life, the route to God; the earliest name for Christians was simply The Way.

We are called to love all as God does sending refreshing rain on just and unjust. But we are also called to direct our love, like God, especially to the oppressed since God weighs in on one side and one side only: against the oppressors and for the oppressed (Barth). Jesus directed his mission to the lost sheep of the house of Israel.

The Committee on Human Sexuality listened especially to the marginalized, such as victims of sexual abuse and of homophobia. Loving God, self, and neighbor sets us against patriarchal injustice. We are called to challenge a society which has been dominated by men. Instead of men intent on scoring and forcing, uncomfortable with feelings, we are invited to redefine maleness in ways more full and free. As women become more bold in naming and rejecting abuse and rape, including date rape---a subject prominent in sociology papers I've read--men will have to turn from sex as conquest to love as mutuality. The liberation of men alongside the liberation of women enables men to own their feminine sides and women their masculinity, both women and men becoming free of confining gender stereotypes and released from the sexism and heterosexism patriarchy has bred. Surely part of love is letting one's neighbor be who he or she is.

3. Scripture Hangs on Love

Jesus and his emphasis on love is the key to interpreting the rest of the Bible. Luther said "Christ is cradled in scripture." We revere the Bible not as an end in itself but because it leads us to Jesus.

Our Presbyterian Confession of 1967 puts it this way:
"The one sufficient revelation of God is Jesus Christ,
the Word of God incarnate,
to whom the Holy Spirit bears unique and authoritative witness
through the Holy Scriptures,
which are received and obeyed as the word of God written."
We start with Christ and his emphasis on love in his life and teaching, move on to scripture, and then move on to the whole of culture, broadly taking in whatever is good there but also judging and seeking to transform what is deficient. The church is not exempt, for "judgment begins in the household of God." I have long been struck by Alfred Loisy's remark," Jesus came preaching the kingdom of God, but what we got was the church." The church is a part of culture, sometimes very much a prisoner of culture, and needs to be reformed in light of scripture, love, and Christ. There are many who have little use for the church but want it to be there in case they drop in on Christmas or Easter or need to be baptized, married, or buried. There are some who don't go to church themselves but drop off their kids so that the children can develop moral character.

There are many who think religion has to do with earning your way to heaven by being good in a narrow sense. There are many who see religion as a source of guilt and condemnation. When I used to do general hospital calling in Missouri, I remember being at cross purposes with some I called upon. I wanted to express love and concern and kindness and hope; they wanted to tell me how sorry they were for skipping church. Somehow the gospel of Jesus Christ with its clear proclamation that there is now no condemnation for those who are in Christ Jesus (Romans 8) has been smothered, and the church has been pressed into the cultural role of upholding conventional morality, perhaps even being bedroom police and liquor cabinet guards. But we should not let culture dictate what the role of the church is. The church can and should abandon the cultural role of moral guardian without abandoning its true calling to be loving followers of Jesus. Being moral is following the mores of a particular society. What the church needs to do--and what the report opens up--is to judge the narrow concerns of morality by the wider concerns of ethics.

It is a pity that the conflict between Jesus and the Pharisees is so often replayed and that the Pharisees so often win! The Pharisees were the moral guardians of their day, sticklers for the law, who laid heavy moral burdens on people but lost all sense of proportion. "They strain a gnat out of their soup, but swallow a camel whole," said Jesus. They tithe mint and rue and cumin and thus keep the letter of the law, but they neglect justice and mercy and faith and thus miss what God requires most. Jesus is incensed by their moralism, legalism, and self-righteousness. Jesus, by contrast, breaks the sabbath law by healing when love requires it, and he teaches that love takes precedence over everything else. Both Jesus and the scribes knew their Bibles well. In Jesus' day, the Hebrew Bible consisted of two parts. The *Torah*, or Law, comprising the first five books, was most important, and the *Nabiim*, or Prophets, contained historical and prophetic books. (Besides these were the Writings, such as Psalms and Proverbs, which were considered supplementary and whose status was not yet settled.) Both Jesus and the scribes could quote scripture, but the scribes just quoted chapter and verse as if all verses were equal while Jesus spoke with authority and not as the scribes, bringing out the inner meaning of the scriptures and emphasizing what was most important at the expense of the less. Jesus asserted that the greatest commands were to love God and neighbor and that upon these commandments hung all the *Torah* and the *Nabiim*, the Law and the Prophets, that is, all of settled scripture at the time.

St. Paul made the same point:

> For the whole law can be summed up in a single commandment:
> "love your neighbor as yourself" (Gal. 5:13).
> He who loves his neighbor has satisfied every claim of the law.
> For the commandments, 'Thou shalt not commit adultery,
> thou shalt not kill, thou shalt not steal, thou shalt not covet,'
> and any other commandment there may be,
> are all summed up in the one rule,
> 'Love your neighbor as yourself.'
> Love does no harm to the neighbor;
> therefore love is the fulfilling of the law (Romans 13:8-10)."

As followers of Christ, we Presbyterians are not at liberty to engage in "proof-texting," which is treating any verse in the Bible as the raw Word of God, immediately and independently authoritative. We believe that a scripture passage must be examined in its literary and historical context, must be stripped of cultural biases we bring to it, must be interpreted in light of the rest of scripture, and must be evaluated in terms of the primacy of love and of Christ.

When it comes to sex, we find a lot of people who are ready to assert that biblical Christianity endorses only monogamous marriage among heterosexuals and who are ready to prove it with a series of passages. What we actually find when we look at the Bible is a lot of things. We find polygamy and concubines among Old Testament patriarchs and kings. We find Jesus being apparently single but blessing marriages. We find St. Paul being single and advocating singleness as superior but saying it is better to marry than to burn with uncontrollable desire. We find prohibition of adultery and of scheming to take over another man's property, seen in coveting his land, house, wife, or domesticated animals.

We find a celebration of erotic love and longing (unrelated to marriage) in the Song of Songs but very little concern with sex as such, except in the context of cult prostitution, which was part of the fertility rites of the Canaanites, who would have a man dressed as a woman engage in sex with another man in order to inspire a local deity (*ba'al*) to fertilize the land. It is likely that this is condemned not as bad sex but as bad religion.

There is almost nothing about premarital sex or about homosexuality with Jesus being silent on both topics. When the sexuality report suggests that masturbation and petting are fine for teenagers but that premature intercourse, unwanted pregnancy, and sexually transmitted diseases are to be avoided, a hue and cry was raised by some churchmen as if the floodgates to sexual license were being opened. But abstinence from sexual expression is not being practiced by teenagers despite the church's apparent endorsement of such abstinence and--in the absence of clear biblical or theological mandates on the subject--it seems better to advocate responsible sexual expression for teens, as for all of us, guided by the tough requirements of justice and love, mutuality and commitment.

There are few biblical passages dealing with homosexuality, mostly misused. A prime example of a misused proof text is the story of Sodom. Here especially we must observe the warning of the Confession of 1967: "The Scriptures, given under the guidance of the Holy Spirit, are nevertheless the words of men, conditioned by the language, thought forms, and literary fashions of the places and times at which they were written." The Sodom story is and should be a shocker to modern ears-- with Lot responding to the threat of having his guests gang-raped by offering to have his daughters raped instead (this is moral?)-- and comes from a cultural context so vastly different from our own as to render it hardly relevant to today at all, much less applicable to loving relations between persons of the same sex. Says the sexuality report (p. 99):

> The story in Genesis 19:1-11 is one of the most commonly used to propose the sinfulness of homosexuality. As one reads the account, it becomes apparent immediately that the demeanor of the men of Sodom was violent. Their intent was to gang rape the guests in Lot's home. In order to understand this text, it is important to know what cultural meaning the writer and readers attached to the violent sexual assault of males by males. In the first place, greater value was placed on a man in that time than on a woman. When Lot offered his two virgin daughters as substitutes for the two men, the offer was turned down because the rape of a man was considered a worse crime than the rape of a woman.

Furthermore, violent and brutal rape was intended to humiliate, and was at times sanctioned for use on a conquered or foreign enemy. In this particular story, the intent was to humiliate and emasculate the distrusted foreign guests, who might well present a threat to the citizens of Sodom. What is condemned in this text is violent gang rape. To say that this account condemns homosexual behavior is to read into the story what is not there.

After dismissing some other passages as also basically irrelevant to today, the report concludes that the main problem with homosexuality is the oppression of homosexuals by society and church. The real sin may not be what gays, lesbians, and bisexuals do in their bedrooms out of love but the loveless way the church has treated them, reacting with exclusion, discrimination, and even violence; only a pharisaic lack of proportion finds the former worse than the latter. The report advocates the full inclusion of homosexuals in the life and ministry of the church and advocates for homosexuals full, committed, disease-avoiding relationships guided, as all of us, by the tough requirements of love and justice.

Conclusion

These issues concerning sexuality are not easy to deal with, but we Presbyterians are proud to belong to a church which is not afraid to raise issues for which answers will be difficult. Our General Assembly wrestled long and hard with the sexuality report, and--though it did not adopt it— it directed the Theology and Worship Unit to include this report with others in study materials for congregations.
And so the debate continues, as it should.
You may have your own current opinions on some of these issues,
    as I have mine, and our views may well differ,
but I hope that you and I—and Christians everywhere--will all agree
    that the primary proclamation of the gospel is God's love for us,
    that the greatest commandments are to love God and neighbor,
    and that everything else is subordinate to the requirements of love.

It's Okay to be Gay: A Biblical Perspective

Right-wing Christians have been infamously vocal in condemning gay people and opposing their rights. Their message, however, is losing traction, especially among younger Americans. A declining majority of Americans think that gay sex is immoral, and an increasing majority think that gays and lesbians should have the same rights as anyone else. Backed by the US Supreme Court decision on gay marriage, it would be possible to argue that gays have the same right to form unions and the same need for benefits. This is necessary but not sufficient. I think it would help to present a Christian position which says it is okay to be gay in contrast to the misuse and misinterpretation of the Bible by right-wing Christians.

When you hear it is wrong to be "gay" or that the Bible condemns "homosexuals," it is clear that you are getting a message from your culture and that the Bible is being misused to confirm cultural beliefs. Neither term ("gay" or "homosexual") existed before the nineteenth century so there is no way the Bible could oppose either as such. This is not just quibbling about words but an opening wedge into recognizing the profound differences between ancient and contemporary culture. The meaning of biblical passages is shaped by the history and culture out of which they came and cannot be applied directly to modern culture without interpretation. New Testament scholar Robin Scroggs concludes his study of St. Paul by saying that he has no idea what Paul would have said about contemporary non-exploitative gay love since it was quite beyond Paul's imagination and experience.

Methodist founder John Wesley advocated supplementing scripture with tradition, reason, and experience. The church, in its traditions and current thinking, struggles to interpret scripture bridging the gap between cultures old and new. Reason resonates with the latest scientific understandings, including the removal of homosexuality from the list of mental illnesses by the APAs (American Psychological Association, American Psychiatric Association). The powerful experience of gay love as godly cannot be denied or discounted.

It is not the case that every scripture is equal in worth. One cannot simply cite a scripture as a "proof text" apart from its context in its portion of the Bible and in the Bible as a whole. Jesus taught that it is important to maintain a sense of proportion, to give weight to weightier concerns for justice and mercy and faith rather than being distracted by minor matters (e.g., keeping laws about tithing spices). Jesus extracted and elevated the commandments to love God and neighbor as the greatest commandments and said that everything else in the Bible (the Law and the Prophets) is subordinate to these. God is love. God does not hate fags, and neither should we. Whoever loves belongs to God.

There are six biblical passages that are customarily used to slur gays: the Sodom story in Genesis, two laws in Leviticus condemning a man lying with a man as with a woman, two vice lists in letters linked to St. Paul mentioning something akin to homosexuality plus Paul citing unnatural same-sex sex as a symptom of Gentile idolatry in Romans. If you eliminate repetition, all of this boils down to four passages. It's not much. And it's not central.

Two of the four passages come from the Old Testament, which is regarded by Christians as subordinate to the New Testament since the new covenant supersedes the old. One is a questionably relevant story about a minor character in the patriarchal saga; the other is part of an abandoned Holiness Code. The other two passages come from the letters of St. Paul in the New Testament, letters which Paul wrote to churches which needed his guidance or expected his arrival soon, letters which the church saved and canonized as scripture because they expressed the Christian gospel despite the limitations of the writer (which Paul himself notes when he wonders if he is right). The vice list in Corinthians is a stock list of vices, and the criticism of the Gentiles in the prelude to Romans is an old standard chestnut; neither reflects Paul's distinctive thinking, and both are tossed out without further development as Paul moves on to his central themes.

What is the sin of Sodom? As a proverbially wicked Canaanite city, Sodom is accused in subsequent scriptures of just about every sin imaginable-- idolatry, rebellion, murder, adultery, covetousness, greed, theft, lying, mistreating the poor, oppression, arrogance, pride, cruelty--just about everything but the homosexuality we focus upon. Long before the heinous night in front of Lot's house, Sodom--a city with less than ten good men-- had a reputation for wickedness, which is why God sent messengers to investigate. The men of Sodom sought to abuse these messengers. Jesus relates to this feature when he says it will be better for Sodom and Gomorrah on the day of judgment than for those who refused hospitality to the apostles he has sent out.

Lot extended hospitality to his three visitors rescuing them from exposure in the public square and giving them the shelter of his roof while the Sodomites, full of hostility toward Lot the foreigner and the strangers he harbored, violently demanded that Lot turn over his guests to them so that they might "know" them. The Hebrew word to know, "yadah," rarely has a sexual meaning, but since Lot counters with an offer of his virgin daughters (who have not known man), it seems to have a sexual meaning here. Captured soldiers and stray foreigners were sometimes gang-raped in the ancient world to humiliate them as losers or intruders. That seems to be what the Sodomites had in mind. Gang rape is wrong, then and now. But to suggest that *all* the men in Sodom, great and small, were homosexual and sought to express their affection for Lot's guests sexually just doesn't fit at all. The Sodom story has nothing to say about gay love though it has a lot to say about those who are hostile and abusive to strangers. Perhaps the true Sodomites today are not gay people but their persecutors.

A pair of laws in Leviticus condemns male-male sex among the ancient Hebrews as an abomination punishable by death. Sounds awful, doesn't it? Yet the Hebrew word "toevah," poorly translated "abomination," refers not to a moral fault but to a ritual impurity, being unclean. Concerned to avoid being contaminated by other peoples, the Hebrews came up with a whole catalogue of abominations.

According to Leviticus, a menstrual discharge is dirty, a woman who menstruates is unclean for seven days, and a man who has sex with her (before she atones for her discharge by sacrificing two turtledoves) becomes unclean. Likewise, a seminal discharge renders a man dirty.

Other discharges from man or woman not only make them dirty but contaminate anyone who touches them, their beds, their clothes, their stools, their saddles, or their spit. Leviticus spends two whole chapters distinguishing what forms of a skin disease (called "leprosy" though not like modern leprosy) are clean or unclean depending on its extent and the color of hairs growing in the diseased patches. To have spots is unclean, but if all your skin turns white, you are clean. To be all of one kind is clean, but mixing is dirty. There are taboos against mixing crops in a field or fabrics in a garment or meat and dairy on the same plate. And there is a taboo against mixing up the roles of men and women in sex. Leviticus does not say it is wrong for men to have sex with each other; it says literally, "With a male you shall not lie the lyings of a woman." It finds male-male sex dirty, disgusting, and abominable because it is confusing, because it is involved in idolatrous religious rituals, and because it is unJewish.

The priestly regulations in Leviticus are designed to keep the Hebrews separate from the Gentiles among whom they live, a people who are holy and set apart, clean before the Lord. Other peoples have other gods, but Hebrews shall put no other gods before Yahweh. Others have their fertility rituals, utilizing male-male sex, male-female sex, and child sacrifice, but Hebrews shall look to God instead for a plentiful harvest and offer God the first fruits in gratitude. Hebrews shall set themselves apart by their dietary laws and by circumcision, but it is not wrong for other peoples not to keep a kosher kitchen or to be uncut. These laws of the Hebrews are for the Hebrews alone and not for everyone.

When Christianity emerged out of Judaism, the Holiness Code of Leviticus was left behind, part of an old covenant superseded by the new. Jesus did not shun lepers as unclean, did not keep the sabbath clear of healing work, appealed to the legally lax "people of the land," and castigated the pharisees ("the pure") as whited sepulchres, clean on the outside but full of dead bones inside. Jesus said that a person is not defiled by what goes into his mouth but by what comes out. Peter dreamed of eating non-kosher foods and was reassured that God had made them clean, and Paul prevailed in a struggle with the "judaizers" in the early church with his view that Gentiles did not have to adopt Jewish customs, such as circumcision, to become Christians. Far from maintaining the old view of holiness as clean and separate, the Hebrew prophets, Jesus, and the early church champion holiness in God and godly people as reaching out, redeeming not rejecting, getting down and dirty in sharing burdens, being all-inclusive in showering grace about.

There may be an echo of Leviticus' male-male sex prohibition in pauline writings. The obscure Greek word "arseno-koitos" (preceded by "malakos") appears in a vice list in Paul's first letter to the Corinthians and is repeated solo in I Timothy, written in pauline style, not by Paul. "Arseno-koitos" is a combination of "male" and "bed" so it means something like "man-bedder" or "man-lier" or "man lying," but it is not clear with whom a man is lying, male or female. One view has the term refer to men who make a living in bed, that is, male prostitutes who service men or women. There is no known use of the term in Greek literature prior to Paul, but the two parts of the term appear next to each other in the Greek translation of the Levitical passage condemning a "male lying" with a male as with a woman, so the term could refer to a male penetrator.

"Malakos" means "soft." If "arseno-koitos" does not mean prostitute, "malakos" may refer to an effeminate call-boy used by arsenokoitai. But "malakos" may just as well simply mean "loose" or "wanton" and not have an explicit sexual meaning, much less a homosexual one.

One reason scriptures cannot stand alone is because they have to be translated. The terms "malakos" and "arseno-koitos" are a nightmare for translators and for those who have to live with their mistranslations. The King James Version did not do too badly with "effeminate" and (the rather vague) "abusers of themselves with mankind." But the Revised Standard Version egregiously presumes a pairing of the concepts and imports alien terminology when it covers both terms with the word "homosexuals" in the 1952 edition and "sexual perverts" in the 1977 edition. The Catholic Church's New American Bible imports even more of one side in the contemporary debate when it renders the pair "boy prostitutes and practicing homosexuals." The New Revised Standard Version (1989) speaks of "male prostitutes and sodomites," which is an improvement though it brings in the Sodom story in a way the text does not and leaves it up to the reader to import whatever sound or poor interpretation is at hand from inhospitable homophobes to would-be gang-rapers to those who engage in anal intercourse (males or females) to faggots. Malakos has also appeared as "catamites" (after Zeus' cup-bearer Ganymede) and "sissies," and arseno-koitos as "child molesters" or "persons of infamous habits."

It is ironic that scholars and translators have spent so much time and energy trying to decipher words in vice lists that Paul may have thrown into his first letter to the Corinthians with little thought. Corinth was a city notorious for its sexual depravity, and Paul is disappointed that in its church there is a man sleeping with his step-mother, folks suing each other, and some men visiting female prostitutes. In the process of condemning these practices, Paul inserts three vice lists, each a little longer than the last with terms in no special order, terms repeated from one list to the others and duplicated in the same list (thief and robber), new terms added; "malakos" and "arseno-koitos" appear only in the third list (and do not appear in a similar list in Paul's letter to the Galatians). In the hackneyed lists, which Paul pulls in from traditional sources, he uses phrases alien to his thought ("inheriting the kingdom of God") and does not expound on any of the vices which happen to crop up. By mentioning "malakos" and "arseno-koitos," Paul does not seem to be condemning homosexuality in general or even widespread classic Greek man-boy mentoring and love but only abuses such as prostitution, exploitation, and looseness.

Paul does muster a whole sentence on the subject in the prelude to his final letter, his letter to the Romans. Although Paul thinks that purity concerns rooted in Jewish law are obsolete, for rhetorical purposes he brings in a standard Hellenistic Jewish criticism of the shameful sexual practices of dirty Gentiles. This gives Jewish Christians in his Roman audience a false sense of superiority before he turns tables on them by exposing Jewish sins. Paul then declares that "all have sinned and fallen short of the glory God intended for them." All of this is just preliminary to Paul's main task of presenting a Gospel of salvation for all through Jesus Christ. Women engage in unusual ("para physen") intercourse, perhaps with men during menstruation contrary to Jewish law.

Likewise men give up customary ("physiken") intercourse with women and are consumed with passion for other men committing shameless ("aschemosyne") acts. Since there is no prohibition of lesbian sex in the Hebrew Bible and hardly any note of it in Graeco-Roman literature, it seems unlikely that Paul refers to it--though he has a rhetorical need not to exempt Gentile women from condemnation and draws a parallel to male activity. Much has been made of homosexuality as "unnatural" citing Paul, even to the extent of holding that there is a "natural law" which says sex organs are made for procreation and must not be used otherwise. Paul had no such notions and, in light of the approaching end time, he does not favor marriage, much less procreation. "Para physen" need not be negative; "para" can mean "beyond" as well as "contrary to," and Paul says that God's grafting Gentiles onto the Jewish olive tree is "para physen," beyond nature (unexpected and marvelous). Paul implies something sordid when he labels whatever women are doing as "para physen" and male-male sex as not "physiken," but he does not use words of moral condemnation but speaks of acts which are "a-schemosyne" (not fitting the usual scheme, inappropriate) and passions which are "a-timias" (dishonorable), a word Paul uses of chamber pots and "unpresentable" genitals, which may evoke shame (but which also may be treated with greater honor).

Paul does not criticize Gentile sexual practices in their own right but as symptoms of idolatry. It is because Gentiles knew God but did not honor God that God gave them up to degrading passions and strange sex as a result of this error. Paul does not predict some awful "penalty" resulting from sexual deviance but sees the deviance itself as "anti-misthos" (consequence) of the error of idolatry. Far more serious, God gave up these idolaters to a base mind and to all sorts of wickedness (a-dikia), which Paul lists (with no sexual sins) and sees as deserving death. Thus Paul disparages the male-male sex he saw practiced by Gentiles in his day (mainly man-boy love) as a minor dishonorable expression of idolatry in a trite rhetorical ploy, which contains purity concerns Paul himself does not share but which helps in passing to establish universal sinfulness as backdrop to the proclamation of the Gospel. This is hardly a frontal attack on homosexuality, and this passage plus three others (and duplicates) may have no relevance to contemporary man-man (or lesbian) lovers who practice hospitality and oppose gang-rape, who find ancient Hebrew purity concerns obsolete, who are not loose or exploitative, and who honor the Creator who made them naturally as they are.

Those who believe being gay is wrong and rummage through the Bible looking for ammunition have very slim pickings. St. Paul lived in a Graeco-Roman culture rife with male-male love and sex. The classic Athenian ideal was a bisexual man having wife and children but directing his main erotic affection toward a youth, whom he would mentor in school and cheer on in nude athletic contests. By Paul's day, there was still plenty of male-male sex, but it had become more decadent with aging perfumed effeminate call-boys on the streets looking for tricks and slaves exploited as unwilling sex-objects and people kidnapped to make them sex slaves (kidnappers precedes "arseno-koitos" in the vice list in I Timothy). Paul may have had these kinds of situations in mind in his off-hand references to same-sex sex, but he would have said a lot more if it had been a major concern.

Those who troll the Bible for pro-gay passages also find little. Jesus had nothing to say directly on the subject. However, according to Matthew, he healed a Roman centurion's gay lover ("pais" could mean "child," but a Roman soldier stationed abroad would not have had his family with him). In Luke's version, it is said that the centurion was "entimos" (very fond, intimate) with his "doulos" (subordinate, servant, slave). Eunuchs were often gay, and Jesus praised those who have become eunuchs (spending pearls of great price) for the kingdom of God. David's love for Jonathan exceeded his love for women, and Ruth loved Naomi so much that she changed locality, nationality, and religion; ironically, Ruth's song "Thy people shall be my people and thy God my God" is often sung at heterosexual weddings by some who would deny any union for gay/lesbian people.

It is okay to be gay. It is neither wrong nor right. It simply is. God's creation underlies all, and the promises of the Gospel are for all. If you are gay, you should accept being gay as a gift from your creator. The Bible has nothing to say about homosexuality per se but lots to say to gay and straight alike about being human, loving, faithful and good. Misled by right-wing haters, the church has allowed itself to get distracted and has done more harm than good; it should support an outcast minority needing justice instead of adding to discrimination, and it should use the gifts of gay people openly instead of spurning them or using them secretly. We can hope that the church will outgrow traditions based on proof-texts and misinterpretation of scripture and pre-scientific understandings and make more of its traditions emphasizing the centrality of love. We can rely on reason to pursue scientific inquiries that will give us a better grasp of sexual orientations. And as those who are not straight (whether gay, lesbian, bisexual, or transgendered) reflect positively on their experience as loving children of God and speak from that experience, we will know more of God's love and grace.

BIBLIOGRAPHY

Boswell, John (1980). Christianity, Social Tolerance, and Homosexuality: Gay People in Western Europe from the Beginning of the Christian Era to the Fourteenth Century. Chicago: University of Chicago Press.

Countryman, L. William (1988). Dirt, Greed, and Sex: Sexual Ethics in the New Testament and Their Implications for Today. Philadephia: Fortress Press.

Helminiak, Daniel A (1994). What the Bible Really Says About Homosexuality. San Francisco: Alamo Square Press.

Miner, Jeff and John Tyler Connoley (2002). The Children Are Free: Reexamining Biblical Evidence on Same-Sex Relationships. Indianapolis: LifeJourney Press.

Scroggs, Robin (1983). Homosexuality in the New Testament: Contextual Background for Contemporary Debate. Philadephia: Fortress Press.

Being Saved by Being Lost (Psalm 22: 14-24; Matt. 16: 24-25; Phil. 2)

The world is full of hucksters. Even religion, which should be holy and unselfish, is simplified and packaged as an easy way to fulfill selfish interests. Beware the salvation-mongers who try to offer you a "deal" on salvation! Some have the audacity to come right up to you and ask, "Are you saved?" The implication is that they are sure that they are saved and are ready to rejoice with you if you are, too, or to get you saved if you are not. After you get past embarrassment at such effrontery, what should you reply? Let me suggest: "No, I'm lost!" Nevertheless, all is not lost. As Jesus says: "Those who save their lives lose them. Those who lose them save them." You see, according to the paradoxical teaching of Jesus, only the lost are saved!

The false answers sound convincing. Pious hokum looks good! And it's so much easier to understand than the hard truth. So we will start with the load of goods about salvation that you may have been sold, and we will see what's wrong with it. Then we will look at Jesus as one who "saved himself" by losing himself. Finally, we will consider what it would mean for us to be saved as losers by putting on such a Christ.

I: The misguided pursuit of salvation

"Amazing Grace" is a favorite hymn of the salvation-mongers. I like to sing of God's amazing grace. But I would like to redo the thinking in one of the lines. The hymn says: "I once was lost but now am found." Let me suggest instead: "I now am lost and so am found." You see, I'm still lost. God's saving me involves my losing myself. On the other hand, Jesus tells us that those who try to save their lives will lose them. That doesn't stop folks who claim to be Jesus' devoted followers from trying to save themselves, however. The salvation business is very much alive. People are eager to pay a small premium for cosmic life insurance if they can save their hides that way. It's very selfish and unchristian. Somehow the idea of salvation got derailed.

The idea of salvation started out fine in early Judaism but got perverted later when it got balled up with an afterlife which one could try to acquire by one means or another. In early Judaism, there was no concern with an afterlife--which promised at best to be a shadowy existence in sheol. Yahweh saved his people by saving them from evil, such as slavery in Egypt, and saving them for good, such as living in a land of milk and honey.

Yahweh made a covenant with his people and gave them commandments to live by so that they could do justice, love mercy, and walk humbly with him. Salvation meant living the good life, which was inherently worthwhile. Salvation was shalom: wholeness, health, well-being, peace.

Yet there was no peace in Zion. Things got off on the wrong foot: the children of Israel fashioned a golden calf even as Yahweh's commandments were being delivered. Israel turned from God, and God turned his face away from her. Assyria was the rod of God's anger. The Israelites were besieged by evil from within and from without and carted off to exile. Israel became a loser among the nations. But the notion of salvation was deepened thereby. Israel had to give up the notion that she had been chosen for success after God made her pay double for her sins since she should have known better. Israel had to scuttle the simple theodicy that only good things happen to good people and to embrace instead the wisdom of Job. And Israel came to the conclusion that evil could not be avoided but only redeemed as she reconceived of herself as the suffering servant of God.

Much of the Judaism of Jesus' day was faithful to this ancient yet chastened notion of salvation. John the Baptist's father Zecharaiah exclaims:

> Blessed be Yahweh, God of Israel,
> for he has visited and redeemed his people
> and has raised up a horn of salvation for us...
> that we should be saved from our enemies.
> He is performing the mercy promised to our ancestors
> and remembering his holy covenant...
> enabling us to serve him without fear
> in holiness and righteousness before him our whole life long...

However, Pharasaic Judaism, at least as caricatured in the New Testament, departs from this understanding of salvation. The notion of a good afterlife as something to be earned had crept in from the peoples among whom the Jews were exiled. And yet the need to resist assimilation into those peoples came to be expressed by excluding them from salvation (as in Jonah's initial refusal to preach to Ninevah) and by emphasizing distinctive Jewish ritual and dietary regulations. Holiness got misconstrued as keeping your skirts clean, and the pharisees were seen as taking a "holier than thou" attitude toward the common people, who were notoriously lax when it came to laws.

Jesus accused the pharisees of trying to make life unduly burdensome for people (in contrast to the easy yoke he offered those who were heavy-laden). Jesus saw the emphasis on external purity as misplaced since the things that defile a person are not what goes in but what comes out of him. Pharisees were smug in their self-righteousness as they observed petty regulations, but they neglected the true hallmarks of salvation: justice and mercy and faith.

St. Paul kept the old view that salvation is a gift of God but with a new twist. In the old view *torah* was God's gift. Paul acknowledged that Law was holy, just, and good, but he believed that humans were incapable of keeping it on their own. They needed an external figure to win God's forgiveness and enable them to follow the law. That figure was Jesus. This "religion about Jesus" supplanted the original "religion of Jesus" (Jesus' own religion). Though I realize that Christianity would probably not have succeeded in the Graeco-Roman world without Paul's transformation of it, I prefer the original. Paul was too much influenced by mystery religions, which present a supernatural savior as an antidote to human problems. He was also too concerned with salvation as afterlife, a concern which gave him credibility in the otherworldly times in which he lived but does not compute in our day. Paul is a great favorite among the salvation-mongers, partly from elements he really added to Christianity and partly from the ways they misconstrue him. We will want to use Paul but do so sparingly; and where the teachings of Paul and the teachings of Jesus differ, I, for one, am going to prefer Jesus.

Medieval Roman Catholicism became preoccupied with salvation as afterlife and provided a definite means to earn it. Heaven and hell were supplemented with purgatory, where most people spent considerable time having those sins purged away for which they had not yet done penance. Grace was transformed into a set of chits by which salvation could be bought. The Lord's Supper, regarded by the early church (and the Greek Orthodox) as the "medicine of immortality," became the conveyor not only of the transubstantiated body and blood of Christ but also, along with other sacraments, of several units of grace. Through his sacrifice on the cross, Christ--plus the saints and all who did more good than bad--made deposits into the "treasury of merit," from which sinners made withdrawals through sacraments and indulgences. Luther castigated this as salvation by works--by ritual works--and was especially incensed by Tetzel, a salvation-monger who hawked indulgences as a way to reduce time in purgatory with the jingle: "As soon as the coin in the coffer lies, the soul from purgatory flies!"

The Protestant Reformation saw life in this world as the arena in which we serve God through our callings rather than just a prelude to an afterlife, and it stressed salvation by grace through faith. But this often gets twisted into salvation by works--by the work of believing. Fundamentalists pride themselves on believing the unbelievable, and their salvation-mongers promise you heaven if you will only subscribe to their creed. Our own Reformed tradition has tried to maintain that salvation really is a free gift from God. Our catechism exalts God's glory above self-seeking when it expects a positive answer to the question: Are you willing to be damned for the glory of God? It agrees with Jesus that seeking salvation is futile.

II: God/Jesus as saved while lost

A Russian anthem proclaims with awe the incarnation of the word of God in Jesus and in Communion: "Salvation is created in midst of the earth." The Nicene creed expresses belief in Jesus Christ as the unique son of God, "who for us and our salvation came down from heaven and was made man." The Gospel of John asserts that "God so loved the world that he gave his son." Although couched in sacramental magic and archaic trinitarian formulae and outdated up-and-down heaven-and-earth imagery, the essential message of anthem, creed, and scripture is that God in Christ lovingly gives himself to us. Also limited in form of expression but even more telling for our purposes is the old *kenosis* poem, which St. Paul includes in his letter to the Philippians. Paul tells us to empty--and thus to lose-- ourselves as Jesus did:

> Have this mind among yourselves
> which you have in Christ Jesus,
> who did not cling to divine status,
> but emptied himself,
> taking the role of a slave.
> Being human,
> he humbled himself
> and became obedient unto death,
> even death on a cross.

Jesus did not try to save himself but chose to lose himself. He did not try to "get to heaven" but chose to leave it. In this the holiness of God is exhibited.

For holiness is not ritual and dietary purity, as the pharisees taught, nor even "moral" purity, as conservative Christians teach, but abandoning purity and reaching out: emptying, humbling, serving, and getting "down and dirty." The holiness of God, as Swiss Reformed theologian Karl Barth reminds us, is seen in the degree to which God condescends to be for us in Jesus Christ--and Jesus tells us to be like his Father: holy, merciful, all-inclusive (*teleios*). God's holiness is not seen in his judgment (though he would be entitled to it) but in mercy: "I am the holy one in your midst and will not come to destroy." As the holy God forgives wayward Israel, so God bids Hosea to forgive his whoring wife Gomer.

As God sends blessed rain on just and unjust alike, Jesus shows us and calls us to a holy love which knows no bounds and spares no costs. Jesus, the wounded healer, makes friends with sinners. He welcomes whores and cheats, such as tax collectors, into his company. He heals people others avoid: lepers, mentally ill, a woman with loss of blood. Jesus is not concerned about defilement or contamination, much less about his reputation. His response to evil is not to avoid it but to embrace it and redeem it, so that being overcomes non-being (Tillich).

The saying is wrong: "Jesus saves"
Jesus never saves; he only spends
      he does not collect a house
            foxes have holes and birds have nests,
                  but this man here (*ben adam*) has nowhere to lay his head
      he does not collect a wife and family
            no one belongs to him but many adhere and follow
            whoever follows is his family--his mother and brothers
      he owns nothing but the ragged shirt on his back
            those with fine raiment are found in palaces
            life does not consist of the abundance of things possessed
            do not gather treasure on earth: prey to moths and thieves
            you cannot serve God and Money
      he has no position
            when called good rabbi, he says no one is good but God
            he is rejected by his hometown church for lack of credentials
                  he's supposed to be a carpenter like his father
            he lords it over no one, including his followers
                  he calls them not lackeys but friends
                  he suggests they will do greater things than he
                  he is among them as one who serves, washing feet

Jesus is a loser
>he loses his reputation because he spends time with those in need
>he loses his audience, who do not understand his teaching
>he loses the good will of the hypocrites he exposes
>he loses his temper when he sees hucksters dominating religion
>he loses his tears when the chicks he would gather like a hen refuse
>he loses his life though crucifixion
>he loses his disciples through abandonment and betrayal
>he loses his God who seems to forsake him

III: Our being saved by being lost

It's not enough for Jesus to be a loser; he wants us to be losers too. He says: "If anyone would come after me, let him take up his cross and follow me." But people don't believe Jesus. They want him to bear the cross alone. They weave fancy atonement theories about how Jesus saved them "once and for all" by his sacrifice on the cross. But no atonement theory makes as much sense as the moral influence one: the cross does not save you unless you are led to repeat it. In the Lord's supper, we repeat Jesus' crucifixion, just as the Catholics say, in an unbloody manner to remind ourselves of the cross which is ours to take up. As wine representing the blood of Jesus is poured out, so we celebrate the pouring out of our lives in helping those in need.

Yet people want to preserve themselves rather than risk being losers. They do not realize that "nothing can be sole or whole which has not been rent (Norman O. Brown)." They want an easy peace of mind instead of an excruciating peace that passes understanding. They want sacraments to convey magic grace rather than to inspire sacrificial living. They suppose Jesus wants worshipers when what he wants is followers. Jesus says: Not those who say "Lord, Lord," but those who do will of my Father belong to God's kingdom. God is not impressed by ritualized sacrifice or sabbath duties: God has no need for them. What God wants is for God's love to be shared. The sabbath is made for humans. It is a special opportunity for relief from work, for rest and refreshment, for taking stock of ourselves, for communion with God and with each other. It is a good time for healing, as Jesus shows. It is a good time for reconciliation before offering gifts at the altar. What it must not be is a religious exercise which tries to hoodwink God and serves as an excuse for evading responsibility. Deeds count, not just a show of faith.

Unfortunately, Jesus never got to read St. Paul so he failed to hear that "salvation by works" is wrong. In his parable of sheep and goats, Jesus teaches that those who enter God's kingdom are those who feed the hungry, quench the thirsty, clothe the naked, visit the sick, encourage prisoners, and welcome strangers. We who belong to God are not to grow weary in well doing but are to lose ourselves and pour ourselves out as Jesus did. That is the road to salvation and happiness. Jesus says, "Happy are the losers:

> the poor (Luke) and the poor in spirit (Matthew),
> the gentle who do not assert themselves
> the kind who spend themselves
> the peacemakers who draw strength from God
> those whose hearts are in the right place
> those who weep in the face of tragedy and misfortune
> those who are abused and persecuted because they stand for goodness

The losers are the true winners. The last are first and the first last.

You hear lots of other stuff. You are told to believe in Jesus and be saved, but it's just "cheap grace" and not the real Jesus who wants us to really follow him. Many conservative Christians have even lined up with those on the Right who say we should save money, lower taxes, and let the poor be damned (they should be "saved" but not helped)! Don't listen to these selfish salvation-mongers. Those who try to save their lives lose them. Listen to Jesus instead. Seek to have the same mind he had and lift him up as your Lord and follow him who emptied himself and took the role of slave spending himself for goodness' sake even though it cost him his life. If you would come after him, lose yourself and take up your cross and do as he did. Jesus' message is this: "Get lost!" Only those who lose their lives in the way he did will find them. Only the lost are saved. This is the gospel: Get lost!

White Racism

It is awful what whites have done to blacks--slavery, segregation, the race riot in Tulsa in the 1920s, the lynchings, filling the jails. It is easy to get white folks to feel guilty or to get defensive. But it is unproductive. Blacks bear the brunt of white racism, but blacks have very little to do with it. White racism is the product of white mentality. Quite apart from any dialogue with blacks, whites need to examine their position and mentality and identity and racism. This is the approach that my colleagues and I took in Project Understanding as we worked with six white congregations in northern California in the 1970s in helping them to understand and counteract their own white racism. It might also help today.

Minister Damon Muhammed from the Nation of Islam said at the mayor's conference on race in Indianapolis that it is wise to build a solid foundation on both sides before building a bridge. He said that he and his organization concentrated on building blacks up. Perhaps whites need to take a similar tack. White folks do not want to deal with race, much less their own racism. It is not polite; they want to rise above race (this is a very "white" attitude and very racist). Some whites look for a chance to "be nice" to blacks and to demonstrate that race does not matter; they are lured by the superficiality and irrelevance of so-called racial characteristics into trying to disregard race as a social fact. Dialogue with friendly blacks can even make them feel better about themselves compared to other white folks. Such dialogue is harmless and perhaps benign but also by itself perhaps premature and an exercise in evasion.

When I lead my session on race in my Introduction to Sociology class, I do not dress up as an African American but as a southern white bigot to portray in somewhat jocular and exaggerated form what racism is and also to show the yankees they are racist too. Typically, white racism has been "dominative" in the south and "aversive" in the north. Whites in the south had plenty of contact with blacks, whom they kept in a subordinate position; whites in the north minimized contact with blacks, whom they ghettoized. Northern whites have preferred to focus on obvious injustices of southern racism while disregarding their own avoidance of blacks.

In contemporary America, north and south, there is more contact between blacks and whites on a potentially equal basis, especially in schools and in the workplace, but most whites and blacks belong to one-race neighborhoods and churches.

Whites do not know what is it to be white. They do not have an identity (though the Klan would like to give them an identity that most would prefer not to own). Dominant groups do not need a distinctive identity; they get to set the standards for all (sociologists call this "ethnocentrism"). White folks do not see themselves as white, but as "ordinary, regular, and normal"-- which is true in the sense that they have the power to set norms.

Being racist is normal in America. Sociologist Robin Williams lists "racism and group superiority" among dominant American values. He also lists "equal opportunity" but with the proviso that we do not expect equality of condition to ensue. Heirs of the Protestant ethic, Americans worship the "bitch goddess success (Wm James)." The American dream is acquisition of wealth surpassing others. Quite apart from personal animosity, racism takes institutional form when whites allocate the best jobs, homes, and schools for themselves while most blacks are left with inferior work, housing, and education. A quarter of blacks (27%) have incomes under the poverty line (compared to 9% for whites), and our criminal justice system is skewed to snare blacks disproportionately.

Perhaps we need to unlearn being white in its typical institutional and personal forms. Assumptions and stereotypes can be explored through such exercises as Man from Mars and "Indian" Poker. In Man from Mars a visitor from space, skin covered in green Noxzema and wearing a cap with curly pipe cleaners in it, probes earthlings about the assumptions they make about race posing Mars as a utopian society with no concept of race. It worked well for me with second graders but bombed with sixth graders bent on unmasking me as a fraud. Like a native American with feathers in his head band, in "Indian" Poker a card is taped to the forehead of each participant, unseen by him, indicating who he is and how he should be treated. Positive as well as negative stereotypes are experienced as restrictive since the multi-faceted aspects of every person are ignored in concentrating only on the trait listed on the card.

Developing greater self-esteem not based on aggrandizement can reduce racism since self-confident people need racism less.

In Eldridge Cleaver's "Soul on Ice" and Joel Kovel's "White Racism," there are useful explorations of the white psyche. Sexual fantasies and stereotypes of white men as administrators and white women as belles and black men as studs and black women as amazons have distorted the relations between races and sexes. Blackness has such a place in the white soul that it is not really necessary for there to be any contact with people called black for it to operate.

In Shakespeare's "Othello" the dark-skinned Othello is portrayed boldly as a war hero yet so mentally deficient and simple-minded as to be easy prey for white Iago's inciting him to fits of jealousy, and what is black is continually identified with evil. Calling black folk "African American" partially overrides anti-black prejudice.

In Project Understanding we tried to move white folks from disabling fear and guilt to activating anger and action. When whites become angry at the way they have been deformed and shortchanged by their own racism, they become ready to dismantle the racist society they have built and replace it.

Kennedy-King Dialogue

King: That was kind of you, Senator, to telephone my wife after I had been arrested for sitting in at a lunch counter in Atlanta along with students from the Student Non-violent Coordinating Committee, whom I joined after it became clear I could not get them to delay the action.

JFK: Well, it was the least I could do, and it almost didn't happen. Bill Hartsfield, the progressive mayor of Atlanta forced my hand. In brokering a deal with Negro leaders for the release of all prisoners and a thirty-day halt in demonstrations while he worked with business and civic leaders to desegregate downtown Atlanta, Hartsfield said that this agreement was in response to my personal intervention. This was not so, but we found a way to make it so. Harris Wofford, my campaign liaison for civil rights, was told by Hartsfield that he and I were out on a limb together so I better not saw it off.

King: Coretta was mighty upset when I was not released with the others but sentenced on a probation violation to six months at hard labor in a state prison. She phoned Harris Wofford in tears. Why didn't you issue a strong statement?

JFK: My hands were tied. In exchange for Governor Vandiver getting you released, I agreed to not make any public statements. But a different approach trickled up from below. Over a beer, Louis Martin suggested to Wofford that I telephone your wife and express my sympathy. When my aides did not answer his phone calls, Wofford passed the suggestion to Sargent Shriver, who approached me when no aides were in the hotel room. I agreed and called your wife immediately.

King: Wasn't there some risk involved? In speaking to the press, Coretta noted that Vice President Nixon had said nothing.

JFK: Sure, there was some risk. When he heard about it, Bobby exploded fearing I would lose the South. But most people saw it as personal rather than political. That's how I construed it when I said: "She is a friend of mine, and I was concerned about the situation." However, the gesture did endear me to Negro voters, including your own father who switched from Nixon to me because I dried Coretta's tears, without unduly alienating white Southern voters.

King: Bobby's calling the judge at Governor Vandiver's suggestion to release me on a $2000 bond was much appreciated. I was deeply indebted to you as a great force in making my release possible. You were really acting courageously upon principle and not expediency. There are moments when the politically expedient can be morally wise. I hold you in high esteem. I am convinced that you will exercise the power of your office to fully implement the civil rights plank of your party's platform.

JFK: That was really Bobby's doing, and I knew nothing about it. But I am willing to take credit for it! Organized by Wofford, the printing and distribution of almost two million pamphlets entitled "The Case of Martin Luther King" to Negro churches the Sunday before the election was beneficial in mobilizing Negro voters to vote for me.

King: During your campaign, you said that it would only take a stroke of the President's pen to end racial discrimination in federally assisted housing. We even had an "Ink for Jack" campaign mailing you pens and ink. Why haven't you issued an executive order?

JFK: I'm a politician. I would not have won the election without the white Southern vote, and the Negro vote provided the margin of victory in Illinois and Michigan. I need both the white Southern vote and the Negro vote to win the next election, which I am fully determined to do. Furthermore, I need Southern white votes in Congress to pass legislation such as raising the minimum wage, which will benefit Negroes. Some liberal-leaning Congressmen have asked me to defer action on civil rights until after the next election lest it hurt their campaign and, if they lose, remove their voice in Congress. I see the Negro making slow and steady progress in areas such as school desegregation and protection of voting rights, and I find civil rights disruptions to be counterproductive and embarrassing to me and to the nation in the eyes of the world.

King: We really cannot wait any more. When I gave my testimony for you in the election, my impression was that you had the intelligence and the skill and the moral fervor to give the leadership we've been waiting for and do what no other President has ever done. Now I'm convinced that you have the understanding and political skill, but so far I'm afraid the moral passion is missing.

JFK: Don't you know that I have done more for civil rights than any President in American history? How could any man have done more than I've done? My strategy in 1961 involves minimum civil rights legislation, maximum executive action. I integrated the Coast Guard on my first day in office. Coming into office, Bobby discovered that the state of Louisiana was withholding funds from three desegregated schools, two of which had been closed down by screaming mobs; as Attorney General he had a lawsuit launched, and the state yielded. I have met with the chief executives of the fifty largest corporations doing business with the government, and within a few months, half adopted detailed voluntary Plans for Progress to hire more Negroes; at Lockheed, for instance, Negro employment increased 26%. I have appointed Negroes to 47 high-ranking positions in government, and am pushing for a Cabinet-level Department of Urban Affairs and Housing with Robert Weaver as its head though I had to delay further an executive order on housing to maintain support for it.

King: It's just like you to take credit for planning to appoint a Negro to a non-existent post!

JFK: Stop them. Get your friends off those buses. Their attempt to integrate buses and bus stations across the deep South is only evoking mob violence. This is too much! I wonder whether you have the best interests of your country at heart. It is embarrassing to the nation and to me as I prepare to meet with Khrushchev over the Berlin crisis.

King: Man, we've been embarrassed all our lives. We put on pressure and create a crisis and then you react. You must understand that we've made no gains without pressure, and I hope that pressure will be moral, legal, and peaceful. Only a creative and non-violent approach can save the soul of America.

JFK: A mob overturned and burned their bus in Anniston, Alabama. In Birmingham, Sheriff Bull Connor let the Ku Klux Klan beat the riders for 20 minutes before intervening. Despite assurances to me from Governor Patterson that the riders would be protected, a state police escort out of Birmingham abandoned the bus when it reached Montgomery, and the riders were again assaulted. I had 500 federal marshals sent to Montgomery, 50 of them protecting you and the 1500 people holed up in First Baptist Church overnight surrounded by a howling mob until Governor Patterson belatedly sent in the National Guard to disperse them.

Without the marshals you would be as dead as Kelsey's nuts by now. Then I worked out a deal with Mississippi Senator Eastland that the riders would be arrested when they reached Jackson for their own protection. You turned down an arrangement where they would be let out on bail. Why?

MLK: It's a matter of conscience and morality. They must use their lives and their bodies to right a wrong. You don't understand the social revolution going on in the world, and therefore you don't understand what we are doing.

JFK: Buoyed up by my presidency, James Meredith began applying for admission to the University of Mississippi in Oxford the day after my inauguration. Defying a federal court order and 300 marshals on hand to facilitate Meredith's enrollment, Governor Barnett blocked it. We negotiated with him to enroll Meredith secretly in Jackson and then he reneged; after that we threatened to expose his secret, and he gave in allowing Meredith to be enrolled. In the meantime there was a wild riot in Oxford in which two died and hundreds were wounded, including 166 marshals. I called in 5,000 federal troops, already on alert, from Memphis, but it took 4 ½ hours for them to arrive in Oxford. I spoke on television that night saying I was committed to maintain law and order though I deeply regretted that any action by the executive branch was necessary.

King: You missed an opportunity to exert moral leadership; you barely mentioned justice. Your clandestine negotiations with Barnett made Negroes feel like pawns in a white man's political game. There is a problem with your priorities. While merely 7% of Negro children in the South attend integrated schools, the major battle of the year is over one Negro in a Mississippi university. Tokenism is a palliative which relieves emotional distress but leaves the disease unaffected demobilizing the militant spirit driving for real change.

JFK: In late November 1962, I finally issued my long-delayed executive order prohibiting discrimination in federally subsidized housing.

King: It was very restricted in scope affecting hardly anyone. The announcement was very low-key sandwiched between a dramatic statement on Soviet bombers leaving Cuba and a major statement on the Indian border conflict with China on the long Thanksgiving weekend.

We've gotten the best snow job in history. We lost two years
because we admired you. We're not going about this right. We've
got to quit begging you Kennedys. We've got to demand our rights.

JFK: In my State of the Union speech in January 1963 I mentioned
voting rights. Saying we are committed to achieving true equality of
opportunity because it is right, in February I addressed the nation
on civil rights as I introduced legislation.

MLK: That did not amount to much. We would have been better
served by your pushing the attempt in the Senate to get rid of filibusters,
which probably would have passed if you entered the fray, and by supporting
a sixth grade education counting as literacy for voting. These moves would
have removed the greatest obstacle to the passage of civil-rights legislation
and enabled many more Negroes to register to vote. I blame this
administration for civil rights running out of steam. The demand for
progress was somehow drained of its moral imperative, and the issue
no longer commanded the conscience of the nation. The time has come
when government must commit its resources squarely on the side of
the quest for freedom. The moral decision is the correct one. I am not
ready to make a judgment condemning the motives of the Administration
as hypocritical. I believe it sincerely wishes to achieve change, but that
it has misunderstood the forces in play.

JFK: We are glad that you waited at our request until after an election
to have your demonstrations in Birmingham though we would have
preferred that you had waited until new moderate leaders were in office
before having your parades, sit-ins, boycotts, picketing, and petitions.
Like the rest of the nation, I was sickened by photos of Bull Conner and
his police attacking Negro demonstrators with beatings, dog bites, and
fire hoses as he arrested 3,300. Yet I lacked authority to intervene.
Nevertheless, we have committed all the power of the Federal Government
to insure respect and obedience of court decisions and the law of the land.
We acknowledge the very real abuses too long inflicted on Negro citizens.
In time steps will be taken to provide equal treatment of all citizens.
We met with business leaders to come to a truce by May 10, which involved
ending boycotts, desegregating lunch counters, and hiring more Negroes.

King: I wish you had endorsed our nonviolent demonstrations and embraced the morality of our cause. I am disappointed with a white moderate who prefers a negative peace which is the absence of tension to a positive peace which is the presence of justice, who paternalistically feels that he can set the timetable for another man's freedom. We're through with tokenism and gradualism and see-how-far-you've-comism. We're through with we've-done-more-for-you-people-than-anyone-elsism. We can't wait any longer. Now is the time.

JFK: After Birmingham I realized that demonstrations would only grow and decided to submit substantial civil rights legislation despite resistance. In an address to the nation on June 11, I said that one hundred years of delay have passed since President Lincoln freed the slaves, but their heirs, their grandsons, are not fully free. Now the time has come for this Nation to fulfill its promise. This crisis cannot be quieted by token moves or talk. I am sending a bill to Congress to integrate public accommodations, hasten school desegregation, and protect voting rights. Race has no place in American life or law. We are confronted primarily with a moral issue. It is as old as the scriptures and as clear as the American Constitution. Every American ought to have the right to be treated as he would wish to be treated. Those who act boldly are recognizing right as well as reality. Though I may not be re-elected, values now mean more to me than votes.

King: Finally, we are on the same page. I hope you will join us in a massive March on Washington when we will have a sit-in in the Capitol galleries.

JFK: Since it looks like I cannot prevent it, I will endorse your March on Washington as a peaceful assembly for a redress of grievances in the great tradition. But let's move it from the Capitol to the Lincoln Memorial and allow me and my brother to supervise every detail of the march to insure maximum safety.

King: The marvelous new militancy which has engulfed the Negro community must not lead us to a distrust of all white people, for many of our white brothers, as evidenced by their presence in this March today, have come to realize that their destiny is tied up with our destiny. Though we face the difficulties of today and tomorrow, I still have a dream. It is a dream deeply rooted in the American dream. I have a dream that my four little children will one day live in a nation where they will not be judged by the color of their skin but by the content of their character.

JFK: When I greeted you and the other march leaders afterwards, I said "I have a dream." We are on the same page. We're in this up to the neck.

King: We felt that the late President Kennedy had been a friend of the Cause and that with him as President we could continue to move forward. I see much more in Kennedy's ability to respond to creative pressure than mere political calculation and crisis-management. He frankly acknowledged that he was responding to mass demands but did so because he thought it was right to do so. This is the secret of the deep affection he evoked. He was responsive, sensitive, humble before the people, and bold on their behalf.

RFK: Martin Luther King was shot and was killed tonight in Memphis, Tennessee. He dedicated his life to love and to justice between fellow human beings. He died in the cause of that effort. For those of you who are black and are tempted to be filled with hatred and distrust at the injustice of such an act, I can only say I feel in my heart the same kind of feeling. I had a member of my family killed, and he was killed by a white man. We can make an effort, as Martin Luther King did, to understand and to comprehend and to replace that violence with compassion and love. Let us dedicate ourselves to what the Greeks wrote so many years ago: to tame the savageness of man and make gentle the life of this world. Aeschylus wrote: "In our sleep, pain which cannot forget falls drop by drop upon the heart until, in our own despair, against our will, comes wisdom through the awful grace of God."

Based mainly on:

Wofford, Harris. (1980). *Of Kennedys and Kings: Making Sense of the Sixties*. New York: Farrar, Straus, Giroux.

Reeves, Thomas C. (1991). *A Question of Character: A Life of John F. Kennedy*. New York: Free Press.

Wolfe, James S. (2013). *The Kennedy Myth: American Civil Religion in the Sixties*, pp. 139-146. Bloomington, IN: AuthorHouse.

Martin Luther King as a Hero for Men

It is a perilous time for boys and men in our society. Our culture has no initiation ceremony by which boys become men, and our notions of masculinity are distorted. One out of three African American males in their twenties is under correctional supervision: in jail or prison or on probation. We need role models. Martin Luther King, Jr. is a hero for men in his archetypal roles of Warrior, Magician, Lover, and King.

Martin was a Warrior, a warrior for peace. He had the courage of his convictions. He did not lie down before his adversaries but stood up to them. He organized movements for racial justice, economic justice, and peace using non-violent direct action. His troops were trained to take blows without either backing down or responding in kind. Through beatings and bombings and torchings and jailings, they were more than conquerors. King was always ready to die and was assassinated in the line of duty while aiding striking garbage men. As Gandhi said, "The path of true non-violence requires much more courage than violence."

Martin was a Magician. He was very learned and earned a doctorate at Boston University. He had a gift for language and a sonorous voice to deliver it. He captivated the hearts of millions with speeches marked by a magical turn of phrase. His inner faith sustained him in a time of great turbulence. He devoted himself to a truth that would set us free.

Martin was a Lover. He was a dedicated husband and father. Though often called away, he stayed connected with his family. His beloved widow and children have kept his flame alive. He was close to his troops and suffered the same blows. He believed in the power of love. He said, "Love is the most durable power in the world. This creative force is the most potent instrument available in mankind's quest for peace and security."

Martin was a King. He was gracious and kind and never condescending. He was as magnanimous in victory as he was implacable in defeat. He sought not to alienate his enemies but to love them and redeem them and join with them in a beloved community. He is ready to shower us with the blessings of his vision if we will take him as our hero and model.

Speech on Just War

Assuming that most if not all of you are pacifists, it is my task this morning to explain and commend just war theory, including President Obama's use of it in his speech accepting the Nobel Prize for Peace. This is a tall order! I'm not sure I want to get you to change your stance, but I would like to shed some light on how the other side thinks. We well may end up agreeing to disagree in a civil and peaceful manner. Coming at peace from different angles need not preclude cooperation. At the Indianapolis Peace and Justice Center, where I have been president for a few years and Ernie Barr served faithfully on the board of directors for several years, pacifists and non-pacifists work together rather peacefully to reduce the amount of warfare in the world and to promote peace.

Before I address the heart of the issue, I want to narrow its scope by sharing some preliminary observations as a sociologist of religion dealing with ideal types in the fields of civil religion and religious organization. An ideal type is an extreme conception or model to which actual phenomena are compared. I will look at archaic, historic, and modern types of civil religion and church, sect, and cult types of religious organization.

I define civil religion as devotion to a nation and its leaders, its ideals and gods, expressed in words such as speeches, songs, and documents and in deeds such as ceremonies, wars, and monuments. The back of your dollar bill (also known as the Almighty Dollar) has our national motto "In God We Trust," the eye of God overseeing our undertakings, and the assertion that a new order of the ages began in 1776; the eagle bears both arrows and olive branch noting that we could go either way toward war or peace. Archaic civil religion deifies the state and promotes holy wars in which the divinely righteous crush their evil enemies. Modern civil religion deifies the individual and promotes wars of convenience to garner resources (such as oil). Neither pacifists nor just war advocates endorse holy or convenience war. This leaves the arena of historic civil religion in which nations and persons are beholden to a transcendent God or transcendent ideals, which not only bless but also guide and judge them. Reinhold Niebuhr saw Abraham Lincoln as America's best theologian because Lincoln refused to assert that God was on the side of either North or South but sought instead to be on God's side seeking to discern God's will humbly as best he could. Our debate is within the arena of historic civil religion.

The basic problem in religious organization is that you can't get everyone to be good so groups have to decide how broad or narrow to be, knowing that if they opt for big, they will have to be lenient, and if they stick to strict, they will be small. At the one end is the church type, which takes everyone in, blesses the world as it is as God's creation, extends loads of grace and forgiveness, and adapts to war as inevitable and acceptable. At the opposite end is the sect type, which insists on strictness, is small, rejects the world as Satan's domain, upholds holy law, and avoids warfare. The religious organization of Jesus and the disciples was neither church nor sect but came closest to the cult type, in which a charismatic leader promises heaven on earth to followers who left all to be with him 24/7 in a total community. When Christianity became the established religion of the Roman Empire, it adopted a church model; monks protested as they stressed strictness as a sect within the church; the Lutheran Reformation stayed churchly with special adherence to the ruling powers (Romans 13); left-wing groups, such as Church of the Brethren, took on a sectarian cast and churchly Calvinists in league with some sectarians as Puritans sought to reform both church and society ["Christ the Transformer of Culture']. Although your sectarian heritage might incline you to a withdrawalist stance where you reject the state and its politics as dirty and satanic and my love for politics might tempt me to a collaborationist stance where I settle for whatever I can get, I presume that we are looking for some middle ground between full collaboration and sheer withdrawal.

Having placed ourselves in the arena of historic civil religion with a reforming stance, let us do three things: look at attitudes towards war and peace in early Christianity, present the just war theory, and watch and evaluate how President Obama uses that theory as well as longs to pursue the non-violence of Mahatma Gandhi and Martin Luther King, Jr.

There is no doubt that Jesus was a pacifist and a non-violent resister to the Roman Empire. Jesus proclaimed God's empire as an alternative to Rome's, and he was executed as a rival to Caesar, the indictment sign on the cross reading "Jesus of Nazareth, King of the Jews." When Peter tried to resist violently, Jesus told him to put away his sword since those who take it perish by it. St. John's Gospel has Jesus tell Pilate that his servants do not fight because his kingdom is not a domination system. Jesus modeled servant leadership instead. He counseled followers to love rather than kill their enemies and not to retaliate against evildoers.

In a supreme irony, the Roman Empire, which Jesus had resisted, embraced Christianity and used it for its own purposes. The church blessed the exercise of imperial power though with some reservations. This was the culmination of a long series of compromises that Max Weber calls "the routinization of charisma," the replacement of extraordinary life with an astounding leader with routines of ordinary, worldly life. In the transition from cult to church, the homeless, itinerant followers of Jesus returned to their families and jobs. The consumer communism in which they held all goods in common gave way to private property. Soldiering became permissible. Christians had refused to join the army either because it involved idolatrous reverence for the Emperor or because they were pacifists or both. The first Christian martyr, St. Maxmillian, was put to death for refusing induction into the army. But now being a soldier who helps to keep the peace was deemed honorable, and war was acceptable.

In a sense when Christianity became linked with the state and everyone in Christendom became a Christian including the emperor, it was inevitable that Christianity would take a more positive attitude toward the state and its wars. After all, the state has been defined, by Weber among others, as the institution which has a monopoly on the legitimate use of force. Even St. Paul, who had no connection to the state, taught that the state is ordained by God to promote the good and oppose the bad, not bearing the sword in vain. When colonial Quakers found themselves responsible for the defense of Pennsylvania, they appropriated money for defense against Indians though, as avowed pacifists, they tried to disguise it as funding for fire stations. The Constantinian church confronted a state which had its own rules for initiating and conducting wars, derived from some ancient practices among Greek city states and the Roman republic and refined by philosophers such as Plato and Cicero. Augustine picked up on these strands and formulated them into a just war theory, not based on Christianity but as the state's best advice to itself exhibiting the approach of the church type, which takes as basic the classical virtues of justice, wisdom, courage, and moderation in the city of man and adds on the theological virtues of faith, hope, and love in the heavenly city of God.

Opening the door to just war does not bless all wars or celebrate war as a good thing, much less as "a force that gives us meaning" in the title of Chris Hedges' critical book. War is always evil, but it may be the lesser evil. In a quotation Jimmy Carter used, Reinhold Niebuhr said "The sad duty of politics is to establish justice in a sinful world."

According to the just war theory, a just war must be just in its aims (*jus ad bellum*) and its methods (*jus in bello*). The criteria for justifying a war include: Just Cause, Right Intention, Last Resort, Reasonable Prospect of Success, Legally Appropriate Authority, Proportionality, Limited Damage.

A just war must have a just cause. It must aim to rectify a situation or hold back an evil aggressor and it must seek an outcome better than the current situation. The Iraq war had a flimsy and shifting set of aims, such as counter-terrorism, preventing use of weapons of mass destruction, replacing a dictator with democracy. Right intention means actually seeking the avowed just cause rather than using it as window dressing for the real goal, which could have been acquiring oil in the case of Iraq. War has to be the last resort after patient negotiation has failed. Yet the Iraq attack was a pre-emptive strike conducted when weapons inspection was not yet complete. A just war must have a reasonable chance of success, something which may be lacking in Afghanistan, the graveyard of empires. Insistence on a legally appropriate authority might restrict warfare to states or restrain a president from pursuing a war without a congressional declaration of war or condemn terrorism, but it might also authorize a subordinate magistrate to buck his unjust superior (Calvin) or a right to revolution (Locke). So that criterion has become murky. Proportionality requires that the injury being rectified be sufficiently grave to spill blood over, that the war save more lives than it takes, that the good of the outcome exceed the damage done. Some people are nuclear pacifists because the damage from a nuclear exchange would be so horrendous. The Israeli incursion into Gaza seemed to lack proportionality because a few deaths from missiles were avenged by a massive massacre. Finally, a just war must limit damage, spare non-combatants if possible, preserve harvests, minimize collateral damage, prepare for a just and lasting peace. Again the Iraq war fell short because military victory was declared in President Bush's mission accomplished speech without any plan for peace.

In his Nobel peace prize acceptance speech President Obama endorses and uses historic Just War theory and in so doing rejects the holy war of archaic civil religion and the wars of convenience of modern civil religion. He says that "No Holy War can ever be a just war," and he goes beyond enlightened self-interest to a universal moral imperative to seek peace. Furthermore, he steers between churchly world acceptance and sectarian rejection by asserting the perfectibility of the human condition and pursuing a world with less war with the zeal of a reformer.

Although Obama justifies some wars, he does so with an "acute sense of the cost of armed conflict" and a conviction that war is a tragic necessity rather than a glorious adventure. He says: "No matter how justified, war promises human tragedy. The soldier's courage and sacrifice is full of glory, expressing devotion to country, to cause and to comrades in arms. But war itself is never glorious, and we must never trumpet it as such."

Obama appeals to a Just Cause as one of the preconditions for a just war. Though he does not explain it, he asserts that "it is hard to conceive of a cause more just than the defeat of the Third Reich and the Axis powers" in World War II. He justifies the war in Afghanistan as self-defense and the first Gulf War as repelling the invasion of Kuwait. He mentions the war in Iraq only to say it is winding down and does not try to justify it perhaps because he thinks it cannot be justified, especially since he might see it failing to be a Last Resort, another rubric of his.

In respect to justice in the conduct of war, the world has done poorly in minimizing damage and could do better in maintaining standards. Obama cites civilians being spared from violence as a requirement of a just war but notes that the "distinction between combatant and civilian became blurred" when "wars between armies gave way to wars between nations," and he rues that in the Second World War "the total number of civilians who died exceeded the number of soldiers who perished." Obama is keen on our maintaining standards of conduct even if others do not: "That is what makes us different from those whom we fight. That is a source of our strength. That is why I prohibited torture. That is why I ordered the prison at Guantanamo Bay closed. And that is why I have reaffirmed America's commitment to abide by the Geneva Conventions. We lose ourselves when we compromise the very ideals that we fight to defend."

While retaining just war as last resort, Obama puts the greatest emphasis on preventing war through international institutions and initiatives, such as the United Nations and the Marshall Plan, providing "mechanisms to govern the waging of war, treaties to protect human rights, prevent genocide, and restrict the most dangerous weapons," a way based "not on a sudden revolution in human nature but on a gradual evolution in human institutions." Obama asserts that building a just and lasting peace would require three things: sanctions for renegades, universal rights, and economic security.

First, applying sanctions against those who violate international law beats having to choose between "armed intervention and complicity in oppression." We can use our power to halt nuclear proliferation, to stop civil wars, to oppose regimes that brutalize their own people, and to stabilize failed states. Occasionally, this will mean sending in UN peacekeepers or NATO troops for humanitarian reasons averting more costly intervention later. Ironically, the threat of force can spur diplomatic solutions.

Second, substantial and lasting just peace needs to be based on "the inherent rights and dignity of every individual" as expressed in the Universal Declaration of Human Rights. Obama asserts: "Peace is unstable where citizens are denied the right to speak freely or worship as they please; choose their own leaders or assemble without fear. Pent up grievances fester, and the suppression of tribal and religious identity can lead to violence. We also know that the opposite is true. Only when Europe became free did it finally find peace. America has never fought a war against a democracy." Encouraging more rights requires not just exhortation but "painstaking diplomacy" and an open door.

Third, a just peace "must encompass economic security and opportunity," freedom from want where people have access to food, clean, water, medicine, education, and jobs including addressing climate change to avert "drought, famine, and mass displacement." Absence of hope can rot a society from within.

Obama ends by expressing faith in human progress, hope instead of despair, and love as preached by Gandhi and King as central. While he does not see the non-violence they practiced as "practical and possible in all circumstances," such as with Hitler or al-Qaida, he acknowledges its strength and moral force. "Let is live by their example," he says, mindful that violence though sometimes necessary "never brings permanent peace," that despite our realism about the world as it is, we can reach "for those ideals which will make it a better place," acknowledging "that spark of the divine that stirs within each of our souls."

Speech on Gaza

Day after day and night after night
we have been bombarded
with appalling scenes of carnage in Gaza,
carnage caused by the illegal use
of planes and weapons
which the United States gave to Israel.
We Americans are complicit;
Our hands are soaked in blood.

This war on Gaza is unjust.
This war is unjust
because it is basically pre-emptive
as it willfully and forcefully brings to a head
a long-simmering feud.

This war is unjust
because the means used are disproportionate
to the provocation.

This war is unjust
because of heavy harm to non-combatants,
including the bombing of a UN school.
Above all, this war is unjust
because it has no reasonable chance of success.

You cannot root out alleged terrorism by terrorizing.
You have to address the root conditions that breed terrorism.
The over-40-year occupation of Palestine must end.
Israel has a right to exist,
safe and secure within its own borders,
and the Palestinians have a right
either to a nation of their own
or to first-class citizenship within a larger whole.
Warfare cannot get us to where we need to go.
War is not the solution;
war only exacerbates the problem
and postpones conflict resolution.

The earliest humans were hunters and gatherers
who cooperated and shared equally and knew no war.
We need to learn from the wisdom of our ancestors.
We need to replace the savagery of civilization and empire
with the mature values of earth community.

When will we ever learn
to pacify our reliance on warfare?
When will we outgrow our addiction to war
as a force that gives us meaning?
When will our Abrahamic religions realize
that our mutuality outshines our differences
as we dispense with separate identities
and in faith do the works that make for peace?

The sordid invasion of Gaza
is occurring during an interregnum on the American scene.
I am hopeful that a new Administration
will address both the short-term and long-term issues.
The war must cease.
The noose around Gaza,
which cruelly constricts emergency food and medicine
as well as impeding prospects for economic development,
must be loosened.
And diplomatic solutions to the Israeli-Palestinian problem
Must be found and pursued
with the determination of the warrior
for the sake of peace.

A Vision of Peace

War is costly and immature. We need to outgrow it. We could
spend our money more beneficially at home and abroad.

We still need the credible threat of war for a while, but only as a
genuine last resort when diplomacy has failed utterly.

Warfare needs to be replaced by policing. Just because the United States
is the one remaining superpower with overbearing numbers of weapons of
mass destruction does not make us the world's policeman. Nations in
concert through the United Nations need to police the world.

The Anglo-American war with Iraq has ousted the regime of Saddam
Hussein in hopes of bringing Western-style peace, prosperity, and
democracy to Iraq. That is unlikely and unwarranted. Despite some well-
publicized scenes of a few Iraqis hailing Americans as liberators, it is
unlikely that we will win "the hearts and minds" of the Iraqis any more
than we did of the Vietnamese thirty tears ago. While replacing what we
have destroyed and providing emergency aid, we should leave it up the
Iraqis to restore law and order, to establish their own government, and to
manage their economy to their benefit, nor ours.

After the diversion of the war on Iraq--which is likely to breed more
terrorists not less--we need to resume the war on terrorism or better yet
make a peace that undercuts terrorism. The terrorists win if they get us
to live and act in panic mode. We need to counteract terrorism at its
roots, not just hack frantically at its branches. Terrorism is rooted in
resentment at perceived injustice and fanned by fanaticism.

The unjust treatment of Palestinians is a sore point for muslims
worldwide. The British established a homeland for Jews in Palestine after
World War I, and this seemed more justified and popular after the
Holocaust. Through early terrorism and later wars, Israel expanded its
territory, occupying the West Bank and Gaza since 1967. Many
Palestinians were displaced from their homes, some settling in refugee
camps. Jewish settlements were established in occupied territory and
prospered while Palestinians suffered. Israeli repression, razing homes of
Palestinians, intafada, checkpoints, curfews, suicide bombings ensued.

If we want to exert power and spend money in the Middle East, let us resolve the Palestinian situation. I envision Jerusalem as an independent international city, capital of no nation (though religious capital for the Abrahamic faiths), policed by the United Nations. Let us resettle the Jewish settlers now in occupied territory in a marginally expanded Israel and assign those vacated homes to Palestinian refugees. Let us establish a Palestinian state independent of Israel though perhaps part of Jordan, which has benign leadership and contains many Palestinians already.

We need economic reform. Communism did not work and has been replaced or revised almost everywhere. Capitalism has triumphed. But it does not work either. Free trade is no panacea. In the global economy, on the whole, rich nations have gotten richer and poor nations poorer. The same is true within our own society. This is not just. We need something different, not only to undercut the roots of terrorism in resentment at economic imperialism, but to establish a more equitable world. Those who work should be paid a living wage, and those who cannot work should be cared for. With Marx I still see emblazoned on the banner of the future: "From each according to her ability; to each according to his need."

We need political reform. Tribal and religious groupings are primary in some places. This often causes strife when diversity is construed as in-groups and out-groups. Nation-states may contain these differences or may succumb to civil war (as in Yugoslavia, Rwanda, Sudan, Northern Ireland, India). One should consider the aftermath before dislodging dictators. The nation-state is itself outmoded. Europe is pioneering regional economic union and government. We need to strengthen world government and protect minorities.

We need ecological reform. We need to reduce dependence on foreign oil, avoid drilling in the Alaskan wilderness, and burn less of the fossil fuels which pollute our planet and produce global warming.

We need religious reform. Divisive and fanatical religions must go. I am working on an alternative. In part it is an historic civil religion, which balances self and society, freedom and order, initiative and equity, unity and diversity, which forges compromises between competing interests, which builds a beloved community during and after the struggle for human rights, which seeks peace with justice.

An Ancient Heritage: Primitive and Archaic Aspects of Communion

A wonderful thing about our modern world is our desire to be unmodern, our yen for the primitive. For years, we measured progress in terms of increasing complexity--more goods, a higher standard of living, and increasing population, a more intricate and interdependent society. But we have found that man--to say nothing of his natural environment--was getting lost in the process. So now our watchword is simplicity. Now we are more concerned for quality of life than quantity of goods, seek to retard if not eliminate population growth, and emphasize basic communal patterns in social organization. Once our slogan ran, "Better living through chemistry." Now we seek to curb the chemical pollution of our environment. Once our slogan was "Onward and upward" as we sought to conquer and harness Nature. Now our movement is inward and downward and even backward as we seek to plumb the depths of what makes human life truly human and to restore men to harmony with Nature. Fads flourish, especially among the young, which feature delving into meditation, exploration of sensitivity, fascination with the mystical and magical, love of earth, delight in light and sound and sense, and commitment to communal styles of life. How appalling all this must seem to the hard-driving, individualistic, rationalistic, puritan culture which we have just left! Its days are numbered and it knows it. There is a new day coming! The scissor grip which the recent past held on us in its conceptions of man and nature and the aim of life is being relaxed, and we are flooded with new alternatives, some of them rooted in our ancient, primordial past, which is now freshly available to us.

It is high time. In the dizzy whirl of our success, we were destroying our world and ourselves. We raped Nature until we produced such a monstrosity we could not bear it. We surrounded ourselves with such abundance until we got sick of overconsumption. And we repressed our natural impulses in our technocratic way of life until they exploded uncontrollably--Nazism, for example, being an extremely logical outcome of our Western civilization. For the basic law of depth psychology is that whatever we repress continues to haunt us and becomes more powerful operating in disguise. The way to health lies in facing and accepting who we are even in our more primitive aspects. Norman O. Brown wrote in Love's Body:

Psychoanalysis began as a further advance of civilized (scientific) objectivity; to expose remnants of primitive participation, to eliminate them; studying the world of dreams, of primitive magic, of madness, but not participating in dreams or magic or madness. But the outcome of psychoanalysis is that magic and madness are everywhere, and dreams is what we are made of. The goal cannot be the elimination of magical thinking or madness; the goal can only be conscious magic or conscious madness; conscious mastery of these fires. And dreaming while awake.

Without going as far as Brown, Harvey Cox has made a switch--or he would say a development--from man the conquering hero in The Secular City to man restored to festivity and fantasy in Feast of Fools.

With this as background, let us take a look at Communion, especially at the "underside" of the sacrament, its primitive and archaic aspects. First, in the face of all that our Calvinist tradition has done to try to spiritualize the Lord's Supper and to deny its ritualistic overtones, I want to affirm its ritual character. Communion is a ritual; it is something we do--together with each other--together with God. Don't explain it. Do it! Let its meaning be in the doing of it. Be faithful stewards of the mysteries of God. Just as a play always means more than our discussions of it bring out, so Christ presents himself in Communion with a depth that our explanations cannot fathom. So be it. In Communion, we are dealing with something enacted on a wholly different level from that of explanations.

The enactive mode of representation is the most primitive and basic in the repertoire of mankind, both as a race and as individuals. Prehistoric man and small babies do not yet possess the gift of language but act out their relationships with other people and with their environment. As we develop, we increase our repertoire but never cease to operate on the enactive level. For instance, we are sensitive to the gestures of others in ways that betray their true feelings more accurately than what they say. Or in the words of a cliche, "Your actions speak so loud I cannot hear what you say." Faith is primarily doing, and worship or liturgy--which means 'work' in Greek--is celebrating what you are doing with your life.

The Sacrament of the Lord's Supper, especially, is an action, a drama, a re-enactment of Christ's offering of himself to be done and participated in and understood at the enactive level.

Continuing development brings in representation on the ikonic level, the level of the great primordial symbols, such as mother, father, earth, sky, birth, death, flesh, blood, sweat, tears. There is power and pathos in these symbols, terror and fascination and delight and mystery. They were forged when mankind or the child was aware of forces in his life he was able to sense but not to control, when wonder was yet alive, when man was groping for the meaning of life, when religion was born. Much of our religion still bears the marks of its birth in ikonic imagery which interprets the acts of God with men with great richness. When we try to discard these symbols as outgrown or to box them in rationally, we find that we have left the realm of experience which religion illuminates. And then we have returned again to the sterilized surface of life devoid of soul where arid concepts reign supreme.

This conceptual mode of representation, which is the highest or at least the latest stage in the development of the child and the race, is no mean achievement. It facilitates the precise use of language, the knowledge explosion, the burgeoning of scientific technology and of the prosperity which it has brought. I bemoan only the ARROGANCE of concepts, the exclusive dominance of conceptual thinking which has been the pride of the last few centuries of our history, much to the impoverishment of man's life and especially of modern religion. If we say that, culturally speaking, God is dead in our era, we are simply pointing to the straight jacket that we have tried to put on God by understanding him only at the conceptual level, where we can still make some abstract sense out of God, but are cut off from sensing him more directly. "The problem," says Harvey Cox, "is that people do not 'experience' or 'encounter' God. Religious language, including the word 'God,' will make sense again only when the lost experiences to which such words point become a felt part of the human reality. If God returns, we may have to meet him in the dance before we can define him in the doctrine." (Feast of Fools, p. 28)

This brings us right to Communion. "If God returns, we may have to meet him in the dance before we can define him in the doctrine." Doctrine, concepts about Communion--whether they be transubstantiation or merely symbolic remembering or sign and seal of the covenant of grace--may have their place (later on), but our primary need is to recover Communion at the enactive and ikonic levels, as the dance, the enacted ritual rife with potent images. Give some rein to your imagination. Be a child in the presence of the holy. Renew the legacy of primitive man which is always a part of us even as we mature.

As Frazer points out in "The Golden Bough," "The Christian Communion has absorbed within itself a sacrament which is doubtless far older than Christianity." Whatever its unique significance, the basic movements in Communion, as in many primitive and archaic rituals, is killing and eating. Baldly stated, the Lord's Supper is an enactment of the killing and eating of our God Jesus Christ. We break bread and eat it. Killing and eating. We pour out wine and drink it. Killing and eating. We say, "This is my body, broken for you; take and eat it." We say, "This is my blood, shed for you; drink it." Killing and eating. In our Scripture, the catechist, disguised as faithless Jews, asks, "How can this man give us his flesh to eat?" The answer is given, "Truly, I say to you, unless you eat the flesh of the Son of man and drink his blood, you have no life in you; he who eats my flesh and drinks my blood has eternal life... For my flesh is food indeed and my blood is drink indeed."

Killing and eating. Death and life. Killing and eating--death and life--go together. Without death, there is no life. This is the fundamental Christian principle. Life out of death. He who loses his life shall find it. The death of the old self and the birth of the new self enacted in Baptism, Crucifixion and Resurrection, the central dynamic in Communion and in all patterns of Christian liturgy and life. Killing and eating. Death and life.

The Lord's Supper is the joyful feast of the people of God, not because death is avoided but because death is included and overcome. Real celebration is not superficial, Harvey Cox reminds us. A full-blooded religion encompasses "tragedy, brutality, chaos, failure, and death, as well as triumph and compassion" (Feast of Fools, p. 23)

The first basic movement in Communion is death, killing, sacrifice. The sacrifice is enacted in bread being broken and in wine being poured out. The use of agricultural products reflects a relatively late stage in the form of sacrifice, but under the surface and through the accompanying imagery the meanings of earlier forms of sacrifice--animal sacrifice, human sacrifice, and divine sacrifice--are carried along.

In terms of animal sacrifice, Jesus is depicted as the lamb who was slain. The incantation, "O Lamb of God, who takes away the sins of the world," is included both in John's Gospel and in the ancient Communion liturgy. It suggests both the Passover Lamb, symbolizing freedom and redemption and the Scapegoat, symbolizing atonement, as well as a whole host of primitive meanings that Freud mentions hovering over the killing of the sacrosanct (animal) victim and the eating of its flesh and blood.

In terms of human sacrifice, Jesus is memorialized in the creed as the man who was "crucified under Pontius Pilate." He is, as the sign on the cross says, "Jesus of Nazareth, King of the Jews," the king who must die, it being expedient that one man should die for the people. Here the myth of the death of the sacred king comes in. In the archaic stage of religion, one step up from the primitive stage, sacral kings emerged to whom was ascribed the maintenance of divine order in their realms by virtue of the special descent from, and incarnation of, the national god. When civil disruption or his own failing health indicated that he was losing his divine powers, the sacred king would be ritually put to death so that his power could be transferred to his successor before it was heavily diminished or lost to the realm. Similarly, Jesus' royal death and resurrection, which we celebrate in Communion, represent a profound threat to, and a restoration of, the rule, order, and power of God.

In terms of divine sacrifice, Jesus' death is portrayed. as God sacrificing himself for mankind out of love. For God so loved the world that he gave his only-begotten Son. God's giving himself is also enacted in Communion. As in the primitive totem feast or in the archaic Aztec ceremony, *tequalo*--God is eaten.

It would take too long to fill you in on totemism, but there is one aspect I want to bring out, the relation of totem and taboo. So far we have been dealing with the underlying meaning of sacrificial killing in Communion in a constructive vein. The Lamb is slain to celebrate deliverance or to gain atonement. The sacred king is killed to restore order. God is killed and eaten--or he gives himself to us, if you prefer--in order that we may share his power. Basically, the killing in Communion is for the sake of the eating. But killing also has its destructive side. In primitive society, there are strict prohibitions, or taboos, against an individual killing a fellow clansman, which the totem animal is, and against destroying the repository of divine power, or *mana*, which the totem animal also is. Yet the community as a whole on a ritual occasion kills and eats that very totem animal--supposedly without guilt. Now it is true that, in contrast to having individuals killing the sacred animals continually for ordinary food, which would tend to extinguish the species, here the animal is killed very rarely and then only to share its sacred powers. Still, I doubt whether sacred blood can be spilled without guilt either in ritual or in the 'justified' execution of a criminal. Freud, indeed, speaks of sharing guilt in the presence of the god as an aspect of sacrifice. He tells a story, which, though it fails as an explanation of the origin of totemism, is very illuminating on the two-sided nature of killing in Communion. In this story, the celebrated myth of the Primal Horde, the sons are jealous of the father's power and his monopoly of the women, so they band together and kill him. And yet, once dead, they proceed to eat the father because they want a part of the power they feared and admire the great man they hated and want to be like him.

It is with some such ambivalence that we approach Christ in the sacrament, resisting yet wanting, killing in order to be rid of him and killing in order to eat him. The Holy always both repels and attracts us; it is, in Rudolph Otto's phrase, *mysterium tremens et fascinans*. In Communion, we see ourselves as Christ-killers as well as Christ-lovers. God sent his Son and we killed him because we couldn't stand him. As tenants in rebellion, we beat the vineyard owner's servants and killed his Son. Whatever Calvary reveals of the nobility of God, sacrificing himself, it also shows humankind--among whom we count ourselves--culpably crucifying its most perfect exemplar. We sit in Judas' seat as well as Peter's at the Lord's table.

And yet the killing is primarily in order to eat. Our cross is bare, representing the overcoming of crucifixion in resurrection. It is the resurrection that we chiefly celebrate in our feasting together on the Lord's Day, life overcoming death. In eating bread and wine, we take Christ into ourselves and gain new life. "He who eats my flesh and drinks my blood abides in me, and I in him," says our Scripture. "As the living Father sent me and I live because of the Father, so he who eats me will live because of me. This is the bread which came down from heaven, not such as the fathers ate and died; he who eats this bread will live forever." This is the bread which gives life, which changes our internal composition, our very being. "*Man ist was er isst*"--runs a German proverb--Man is what he eats. In Communion, we eat Christ and become what we have eaten. We not only receive the Body of Christ, but in so doing we become the Body of Christ. Christ incarnates himself through bread and wine in us, and we incorporate him into ourselves. God becomes man that man may become God--in living communion. And the life of God in which we participate we share together; we become together--corporately--the Body of Christ. Just as with the primitives, feasting on God binds us together. Like the Bedouins who eat in friendship, sharing Christ's blood makes us blood-brothers. In Christ's blood, there is a new covenant. In Christ, we are, together, a new creation.

It has been a long journey that we have undertaken with much that is strange and new in its very ancientness. You may be a little confused. We have barely scratched the surface of the range and depth of meanings in Communion. We noted how man's frantic penchant for accumulation is giving way to a search for soil in which to restore his soul. We have seen how willingness to operate at enactive and ikonic levels rather than exclusively at the conceptual level is essential to this restoration. And we have looked at Communion, both in its primitive and archaic underpinnings and in the historic Christian meanings which have overlaid them, both in terms of its enactment of killing and eating and in its ikonic significance of death and life. I am not advising you to think of all these things while you take Communion. Don't think about it. Do it. But in doing it, be open to the deeper levels of meaning which come to you even if they seem childish or primitive or only barely conscious. Feel free! And be open to the Spirit of Christ presenting itself in Communion, the spirit that gives life in spite of death and makes us one.

Spectator Sports as a Religion

A spectre is haunting America. There is an invisible religion at work though it is in plain view. It is spectator sports.

Q. How can this be? Sports are just play.
A. Hardly. Spectator sports is a serious multi-billion-dollar business. Televised sporting events, including pre-game and post-game shows, draw huge audiences, and a good portion of nightly TV "news" is devoted to sports. The highest-priced commercials occur during half time at the Super Bowl. Whole sections of newspapers feature sports, and these widely-read sections sell newspapers. Sports dominate male conversation, and many men and boys can cite statistics, chapter and verse, about well-publicized athletes. Like the *Torah* of old, sports insignia adorn the persons and dwelling of devotees. Large cities vie to attract professional teams and spend public funds to build lavish stadiums (perhaps today's cathedrals); collegians identify themselves by their sports mascots and rally around their teams; almost everyone in some small towns turns out to cheer on their high school athletes; suburban women who drive their wee ones to sports practice and performance are tagged in the media as "soccer moms." The sports empire extends from professional athletes paid obscenely high salaries at the top of the food chain down through collegiate and high school jocks to tiny tots in Little Leagues.

Q. How important is spectator sports at each of these levels?
A. Professional athletes are celebrities serving as role models for kids. Collegiate athletes at the top schools (i.e., schools which perform best at sports, a criterion which far outshines academics in rating schools) are paid to work at their sports though scholarships. The claim to fame of many small towns rests on sports performance: the sign as you drive into the town regales an athletic contest their high school team won in some year (e.g. Bear Lake, Michigan). Amid the diversity of ecclesiastical religions, schools drum up a unifying "school spirit" as a religion aimed at supporting sports teams (instead of holy spirit). Jocks are idolized. From a tender age, boys who do not perform well at sports are labeled as sissies, and their lives are often a living hell. The boys who shot up Columbine High School did so in part out of resentment at the jocks who made their non-athletic lives miserable.

Q. So spectator sports is important. But what makes it a religion?
A. Whatever a person is most devoted to is their god, said Luther. Fans get plenty passionate about their teams and astonish me with all the time and talk they waste on the sporting events they watch. There are ceremonies involved with sports as with churches, especially at the Olympics, and there are codes of conduct for athletes. There is a common element of play in church or sport: the priest is the celebrant, the chief player, and top athletes are celebrities.

Q. What kind of religion does spectator sports most closely resemble?
A. It is closest to primitive religion. Both involve escape from the mundane into sacred time and space. There is noise, excitement, enthusiasm, intoxication, and even breaking taboos, whether incest at the corrobbori or baring breasts at the Indy 500. Just as the American flag serves as a totem for civil religion, sports flags/logos are totems.

Q. Do churches recognize spectator sports as a rival religion?
A. No. Spectator sports is a sacred cow. I have heard criticism of those who play golf on Sundays instead of church but never heard spectator sports criticized in church. I have heard lots of analogies in sermons based on sports and even heard a prayer in an Indy church for Pacer victory. Ministers know not to speak long when there's a game to watch. My younger son does not attend church but goes to Raiders' games religiously and surrounds himself with Raiders totems.

Q. Marriage is a sacred institution. Can spectator sports compete?
Many men are more married to TV than to their wives when Sunday or Monday night football is on. They bond with male watchers more than wives.

Q. How did you notice this?
A. I am an American by birth, not by fealty. I observe culture with a jaundiced and amused eye. I hardly ever watch spectator sports. Marginality breeds insight. I have been the odd man out in countless male conversations at lunch since I have no idea what is going on in the world of spectator sports. This accents how crucial it is to others.

Q. Have others noticed spectator sports as a religion?
A. Without systematic analysis, journalists have used religious images in describing sports. For instance, articles have depicted a sports arena as "hallowed ground" and noted the "worship" of sports heroes. Sociologists report that TV time exceeds school time, have seen blacks and women assault the white male priesthood of sports players (not owners/coaches), and see harm in seeking to be a professional athlete.

Q. Are you opposed to sports?
A. No. Playing is good for people and so is exercise. I am active in tennis, bicycling, and golf preferring to spend my sports time playing rather than watching. In spectator sports, someone else works rather than plays, and the viewer exercises ears and eyes if media-hooked (or stands up and yells in the stands). Like most idolatry, sports is good in its place and bad as a religion. Team sports teach cooperation among friends in opposition to the enemy; Max Rafferty, former California superintendent of instruction, said that football is the best preparation for war. The cult of winning, the ethic of competition, and worship of what William James called "the bitch goddess" Success is reinforced by sports. Pedaling my bicycle at a leisurely pace with friends on a charity fund-raiser has a more benign ambience, I think.

Life Eternal

The biblical saga runs from Creation to Last Judgment. In the language of myth, what is primarily true is put at the beginning, and what is finally true is put at the end. But in actuality these truths do not apply to times and climes remote but to the one life each of us leads between birth and death in the here and now. Adam is not the proper name of a primeval progenitor but the generic name of every human earthling. Man is called Adam because he comes from "adamah," the ground. God takes dirt and blows into it the breath of life, and each of us becomes "nephesh hayah," a living creature, like all the other animals. From dust we come, and to dust we return when we have breathed our last.

God's judgment is not postponed but comes now, negatively as Hebrew prophets taught, on those who trample upon the poor, and positively as Jesus taught, on those who feed the hungry, quench the thirsty, clothe the naked, and visit the sick and those in prison. The message remains: The empire of God is at hand; change your mind, and believe this good news. The blind see; the sick are healed; the oppressed go free; the demons are expelled. Satan like lightning falls from heaven. The wish is that the demonic legions of imperial soldiers would rush as pigs to drown in the sea. If by God's power, demons are cast out, then is God's empire come in our midst. This is the judgment: that light came into the world, but men preferred darkness. But those who lose their lives for the sake of God's rule find their lives enveloped in the eternal mission of God.

Lives begin and expire. Relationships come and go. Ecstasies spiritual and sexual flare up and subside. Craving for immortality and everlasting love and endless bliss increase our suffering according to the Buddha. Better to accept life as it is, to follow the flow. All things come from Tao and return to it. Tao in the world is like a river flowing home to the sea. I accept and revel in my human, mortal life in my poem "No Trace:"

> Ashes to ashes and dust to dust,
> I came when I might and left when I must.
> Walked I softly and made no dent,
> In joy and peace my years were spent.
> I lived in love and cast out fear;
> I came, I saw--and then I went.

Some crave more. Heaven, an afterlife, a second life. A metaphysical immortal soul inhabiting a mortal body. Reincarnation. Resurrection. But I have no need or desire for a second life. What I have and seek, and to which I see these extensions point, is an affirmation of my one embodied life as everlasting, not in duration but in significance.

Like all creatures, we are embodied and aware. In Whitehead's terms there is a physical and a mental pole in every actual entity, in every cell, and in that integral phenomenon which physically we call the brain and mentally we call the mind. The brain is an instrument on which mind plays, developing more neural pathways where it is used more, and the brain facilitates consciousness, self-consciousness, mindfulness, meditation. A missing part of the brain can mean a missing part of the mind though our resilient brains can sometimes take up the slack elsewhere. However, a dead brain and body mean no mind and no means to communicate.

Though literally impossible, the resurrection of the body for Jesus and for ourselves affirms the value and impact of actual lives. Jesus gets his same body back, wounds and all. Jesus eats fish, breaks bread, passes through walls, ascends to the sky. The peculiarity of these stories shows they are metaphor. Jesus up equals Spirit down. The Spirit of God, which coursed through Jesus, blows through us. The Word of God, spoken by the prophets, became flesh in Jesus and continues: God is still speaking. Jesus is really dead, but he influences those who follow him; discipleship is the way in which Jesus' life is extended, an extension of the incarnation. When we evoke the mind of Christ as guide or guru, we resurrect his consciousness and empower our own. Love we embody keeps flowing.

Our lives are hid with Christ in God. In Whitehead's terms, God prehends and preserves the life of all creatures in God's mind, and creatures choose among the lures for feeling he provides to build a world that shapes God. We are co-creators with God, and man's participation in the creativity of God is man's dignity and grandeur, relegating the question of personal immortality to irrelevancy. We experience life eternal when we interact with, and are drawn into, the eternal life of God. As in my poem "Alison," the transience of beauty and of our lives do not diminish their worth.

> The God-breath comes to life in us,
> And we though mortal live eternally in time,
> And God's own life transfigures us sublime.

Addendum: Reflexive Statement

It is the custom in presentations at Association for Humanist Sociology meetings to provide a reflexive statement indicating how you are personally involved in the subject being researched and enacted. Before a presentation on a Voter Registration Project, which had students in my introductory sociology course locating and canvassing apartments in low-income areas, I had this to say about my engagement:

An Eastern philosopher wondered
if he was a human dreaming he was a butterfly
or a butterfly dreaming he was a human.
I wonder if I am an activist who teaches or a teacher who is an activist.
I have never not taught
even when my day job was being a computer programmer.
I have always been an activist
with civil rights being prime
when I worked for a black Baptist church in inner-city Cleveland
and opposition to the Vietnam War taking center stage
when I was a grad student in Berkeley
and many issues taking the limelight
when I was president of the Indianapolis Peace and Justice Center.

I have a friend whose son used to enjoy telling people
"My dad sleeps with men for money."
His father was a paid caregiver on an overnight shift then,
but now he is an international human rights lawyer.
He switched from service to justice.
I find most standard service-learning projects to be wanting
because they supplement failed systems with charity,
such as recreational activities for children,
rather than seeking justice by transforming failed systems.
Children are not the hope for tomorrow because they become adults;
we need to empower adults to fix the world we have messed up.
Like Martin Luther King, Jr., I try to be drum major for justice,
sounding, as he did, the call of the prophet Amos who sees God saying:
"Take away from me the noise of solemn assemblies; to the
melodies of your harps, I will not listen. But let justice run down
like waters and righteousness like a mighty stream."

64963779R00064

Made in the USA
Lexington, KY
26 June 2017